DEDALO /

AMSTERDAM

Travel guide

HOW TO PLAN
A TRIP TO AMSTERDAM
WITH BEST TIPS
FOR FIRST-TIMERS

Edited by: Domenico Russo and Francesco Umbria
Design e layout: Giorgia Ragona
Book series: Journey Joy

Amsterdam Travel guide
How to Plan a Trip to Amsterdam
with Best Tips for First-Timers

www.agenziadedalo.it

AMSTERDAM

Travel guide

Foreword

In the following pages of the book, you will find essential advice on what to see and do in Amsterdam, and there will be specific insights to enjoy your trips to the fullest (even without spending exorbitant amounts).

The travel guide series of the Journey Joy collection was designed to be lean and straight to the point. The idea of keeping the guides short required significant work in synthesis, in order to guide the reader towards the essential destinations and activities within each country or city.

If you like the book, leaving a positive review can help us spread our work. We realize that leaving a review can be a tedious activity, so we want to give you a gift. Send an email to **bonus@dedaloagency.net**, attach the screenshot of your review, and you will get completely **FREE**, in your mailbox, **THE UNRELEASED EBOOK**: "The Art of Traveling: Essential Tips for Unforgettable Journeys".

Remember to check the Spam folder, as the email might end up there!

We thank you in advance and wish you to always travel and enjoy every adventure!

Index

Introduction

Welcome, dear traveler, to your indispensable guide to exploring the enchanting city of Amsterdam! A place where history is reflected in the shimmering canals, where vibrant tulips breathe life into the cityscape, and where gezelligheid (coziness) is not just a word, but a way of life.

In this guide, we set sail on a journey through this city of tales, uncovering the secrets that make Amsterdam a destination of eternal allure. Let's embark on an adventure that will etch memories on your soul. This journey to Amsterdam will stay with you not just in photos and souvenirs but in the life-altering experiences and memories that will inspire stories worth recounting.

Chapter 1 introduces you to the heart of the Netherlands, Amsterdam Central. This area effortlessly blends the past and the present into a lively mix that is uniquely Dutch. As you navigate through Amsterdam Central, the majesty of the Royal Palace and the historic Amsterdam Centraal Station will leave you spellbound. Wander through the bustling Dam Square, delve into the profound history that every corner of the city murmurs, and let your taste buds dance in the culinary delights unique to the Netherlands.

Our journey then meanders through the pages of history in Chapter 2. The iconic Anne Frank House, the majestic Rijksmuseum, and the vibrant Rembrandt House Museum are just a few of the treasures you will unearth.

Chapter 3 is dedicated to the artistic soul of Amsterdam. Wander through the illustrious Van Gogh Museum, admire contemporary art at the Stedelijk Museum, and immerse yourself in the city's thriving music scene.

Next up is modern Amsterdam, covered in Chapter 4. It offers a unique blend of innovative architecture, technological marvels, and sustainable initiatives. From the A'DAM Lookout to the innovative IJburg, Amsterdam is a city that never ceases to amaze.

In Chapter 5, we explore the delightful world of Dutch cuisine. This journey will take you through the world of Dutch cheese, the comforting embrace of stroopwafels, and the refreshing taste of local beers and jenever.

Chapter 6 invites you into the world of shopping in Amsterdam. From the bustling flea markets to the chic boutiques and antique shops, Amsterdam offers a shopping experience like no other.

Amsterdam's vibrant nightlife takes center stage in Chapter 7. Experience the warmth of the brown cafés, the energy of the nightclubs, and the creativity of the city's theatre and performance scene.

In Chapter 8, we take you off the beaten path to discover the hidden gems of Amsterdam. From the tranquil Amsterdamse Bos to the quirky De Pijp, there is a world waiting to be discovered beyond the tourist trails.

Chapter 9 immerses you in the changing seasons of Amsterdam. Experience the city in bloom during spring, bask in the summer sun, marvel at the autumnal hues, and embrace the cozy winter vibes.

As we delve into Chapter 10, you will find a practical guide to experiencing Amsterdam on a budget. This chapter equips you with valuable insights on affordable accommodation, dining, and transportation options.

In Chapter 11, we immerse you in the cultural experiences you must try in Amsterdam. Imagine participating in a traditional Dutch cooking class or joining a cycling tour through the city's iconic canal ring.

Our Amsterdam exploration culminates in Chapter 12, where we guide you through the most scenic walks and bike rides in the city. From the historic Canal Ring to the vibrant De Pijp, each route offers a unique perspective on Amsterdam.

This guide is not just a roadmap to the physical landscapes of Amsterdam. It's an invitation to journey through a captivating world of rich history, vibrant culture, delicious cuisine, and breathtaking natural beauty. As you embark on this journey, you'll find Amsterdam revealing its heart and soul to you, letting you in on its secrets, traditions, and the indomitable Dutch spirit. In the end, you'll leave Amsterdam with a piece of it etched in your heart, only to return again and again to discover more of what this incredible city has to offer. Let's go – your Amsterdam adventure awaits!

CHAPTER 1:
Amsterdam Central
· ·

Entering Amsterdam is like stepping into a world where the past and the present collide in the most beautiful way. The capital of the Netherlands, Amsterdam is a city of canals, historic buildings, world-renowned museums, and vibrant neighborhoods. It's a city that invites you to explore its charming streets, savor its rich culinary offerings, and immerse yourself in its captivating culture. At first glance, Amsterdam enchants with its iconic canal houses, historic bridges, and the network of canals that define its landscape. Yet, Amsterdam is more than just its picturesque facade. It is a city that embraces innovation while preserving its rich history, where historic buildings house cutting-edge enterprises, and where centuries-old traditions coexist with contemporary art and culture.

As we journey together through Amsterdam's rich tapestry, you will get to experience firsthand the city's timeless allure. We'll traverse its historic center, visit its renowned museums, and explore its lively neighborhoods. You'll learn how the Amsterdammers enjoy their local culinary delights, how they entertain, and how they balance modern living with a deep respect for their past. You'll see how history and modernity coalesce in this metropolis, making Amsterdam a city like no other.

So, let's put on our walking shoes, adjust our sun hats, and dive headfirst into the fascinating world of Amsterdam - the city that always was, and always will be, a symbol of innovation, tolerance, and beauty.

The Dam Square

Our journey begins at Dam Square, the historic heart of Amsterdam. This bustling square, surrounded by some of the city's most iconic buildings, is a microcosm of Amsterdam's history and its contemporary vitality. The Royal Palace, the Nieuwe Kerk (New Church), and the National Monument all tell stories of the city's past, while the street performers, vendors, and lively atmosphere reflect its modern-day vibrancy.

Stand in the center of the square and let your gaze wander over the stunning architecture that surrounds you. Picture the historic events that have taken place here, from royal inaugurations to protests and celebrations. Imagine the people who have stood where you stand, from kings and queens to ordinary citizens, all contributing to the rich tapestry of Amsterdam's history.

As you navigate through the square, take note of the various activities available. Enjoy a coffee in one of the many cafés lining the square, visit the Royal Palace or the Nieuwe Kerk, or simply sit and people-watch, absorbing the atmosphere of this lively meeting place. Remember, Dam Square is not just a historic site; it's a living, breathing part of the city, and to fully appreciate its charm, you must immerse yourself in its rhythm.

Rijksmuseum

Next, we head to the Rijksmuseum, one of the world's most famous art museums. Home to a vast collection of art and historical artifacts, the Rijksmuseum is a treasure trove of Dutch history and culture. From the masterpieces of Rembrandt and Vermeer to the intricate works of Dutch decorative arts, the museum offers a comprehensive overview of the Netherlands' artistic and cultural heritage.

As you wander through the museum's galleries, allow yourself to be transported back in time. Admire the intricate details of the masterpieces on display, and imagine the artists who painstakingly created them. Consider the historical events that shaped the art and artifacts you see before you, and reflect on the role they played in shaping the Netherlands as we know it today.

Before you leave the museum, take a moment to visit the Rijksmuseum's beautiful gardens. Relax by the pond, admire the sculptures, and soak in the peaceful atmosphere. And remember, the Rijksmuseum is not just a museum; it's a gateway into the Netherlands' rich cultural heritage. To truly appreciate its offerings, take your time, explore its many galleries, and allow yourself to be transported into the world of Dutch art and history.

Van Gogh Museum

Our next stop is the Van Gogh Museum, home to the world's largest collection of works by Vincent van Gogh. This museum, dedicated to one of the most famous and influential figures in the history of Western art, offers a unique opportunity to see the evolution of Van Gogh as an artist and to understand the struggles and triumphs that shaped his life and work.

As you explore the museum, allow yourself to be captivated by the vibrant colors, bold brushstrokes, and emotional intensity of Van Gogh's paintings. From his early works, which reflect the somber tones of his Dutch heritage, to his later works, which burst with color and light, the museum provides a comprehensive overview of Van Gogh's artistic journey.

Before you leave the museum, take a moment to reflect on the life and legacy of Vincent van Gogh. Consider the challenges he faced, the innovations he brought to art, and the impact his work has had on artists and art lovers around the world. And remember, the Van Gogh Museum is not just a collection of paintings; it's a testament to the enduring power of art to reflect and transform our lives.

Anne Frank House

Our journey continues at the Anne Frank House, a museum dedicated to the Jewish girl who went into hiding with her family during the Second World War and wrote a diary that would become one of the most famous and poignant accounts of the Holocaust. Located in the building where Anne and her family hid for more than two years, the museum offers a powerful and moving experience.

As you tour the museum, you will see the actual hiding place where Anne and her family lived in fear and uncertainty. You will see the original diary that Anne wrote during her time in hiding, and you will learn about the people who helped the Frank family and the tragic outcome of their story.

Before you leave the Anne Frank House, take a moment to reflect on the lessons of Anne's story. Consider the courage it took for her and her family to go into hiding, the resilience she showed in the face of adversity, and the importance of standing up against injustice. Remember, the Anne Frank House is not just a museum; it's a reminder of the human capacity for hope and resilience, even in the darkest of times.

Canal Cruise

No visit to Amsterdam would be complete without a canal cruise. The city's canals, a UNESCO World Heritage site, offer a unique perspective on Amsterdam's history and architecture. As you glide along the water, you'll see iconic landmarks, picturesque bridges, and charming canal houses, all while learning about the city's fascinating history.

As you embark on your canal cruise, allow yourself to relax and take in the sights. Enjoy the fresh air, the gentle lapping of the water against the boat, and the picturesque views that unfold before you. Consider the history of the canals, which were constructed in the 17th century and played a crucial role in Amsterdam's development as a major trading city.

Before your cruise ends, take a moment to appreciate the beauty and tranquility of the canals. Consider how they have shaped and defined Amsterdam over the centuries, and how they continue to be a vital part of the city's identity. Remember, a canal cruise is not just a tourist activity; it's a chance to connect with the essence of Amsterdam and to see the city from a unique vantage point.

Red Light District

The next stop on our journey is the infamous Red Light District, one of the most talked-about neighborhoods in Amsterdam. Known worldwide for its red-lit windows, coffeeshops, and open-minded approach to sex and cannabis, the Red Light District represents a facet of Dutch culture that many find intriguing, yet others controversial.

As you wander through its narrow, cobblestone streets, you'll encounter a world unlike any other; a place where the norms of everyday life seem to be turned on their head. Amidst the buzz of activity, you might catch a glimpse of a moment in time, frozen within the confines of a window frame, or the wafting aroma of cannabis escaping from a nearby coffeeshop.

However, it's important to approach this area with sensitivity and respect. Remember that the women working in the windows are professionals, and it is important to treat them with dignity and respect. Also, while cannabis is tolerated in coffeeshops, it is illegal to consume it in public places. Before venturing into the Red Light District, take a moment to reflect on your own boundaries and the local customs and laws. Remember, the Red Light District is not just a tourist attraction; it's a living, breathing neighborhood with its own rules and rhythms.

The Royal Palace

Continuing on our journey, we arrive at the Royal Palace, an imposing structure that stands as a testament to Amsterdam's rich history and its enduring importance as a European capital. Originally built as a town hall in the 17th century, the Royal Palace has been the official residence of the Dutch monarch since 1808. As you approach the palace, take a moment to appreciate its grand façade, a masterpiece of classical architecture.

While the palace is still in use by the Dutch royal family, it is open to the public for most of the year. As you tour the interior, you'll be captivated by the sumptuous furnishings, intricate carvings, and magnificent paintings that adorn its halls. Each room tells a story, from the grandeur of the Citizens' Hall, with its marble floor and intricate maps of the world, to the intimate chambers of the royal family. Before leaving the Royal Palace, take a moment to reflect on its historical significance and its role in the modern-day Netherlands. Consider the challenges and triumphs of the Dutch nation, and how the Royal Palace stands as a symbol of both its past and its present. Remember, the Royal Palace is not just a historic building; it's a living symbol of the Dutch nation.

Vondelpark

Our final stop is the Vondelpark, a lush, sprawling oasis in the heart of Amsterdam. Named after the famous Dutch playwright Joost van den Vondel, the park is a beloved retreat for both locals and visitors alike. As you stroll along its winding paths, you'll encounter tranquil ponds, beautifully landscaped gardens, and art installations that add a touch of whimsy to the natural surroundings.

The Vondelpark is also a hub of activity, with open-air concerts, theatre performances, and outdoor exercise classes taking place throughout the year. Whether you're looking to relax and unwind or to engage in some physical activity, the Vondelpark offers something for everyone. Before leaving the Vondelpark, take a moment to appreciate the beauty of nature and the importance of public spaces in urban environments. Consider the role that parks like the Vondelpark play in fostering community and promoting well-being. Remember, the Vondelpark is not just a park; it's a vital part of the social fabric of Amsterdam.

Dutch Cuisine

The culinary scene in Amsterdam is as diverse as its population, but it's important not to overlook traditional Dutch cuisine.

Dutch food is hearty and wholesome, with key ingredients including potatoes, vegetables, meat, and fish. One of the most popular traditional dishes is 'stamppot', a mashed mixture of potatoes and vegetables, usually served with a sausage. Another classic dish is 'haring', raw herring fish typically served with onions and pickles. For those with a sweet tooth, 'stroopwafels', caramel-filled waffles, and 'poffertjes', mini pancakes, are a must-try.

Amsterdam is also home to a variety of international cuisines, from Indonesian to Moroccan, reflecting its multicultural heritage. As you explore the city, take the time to savor its culinary delights. Whether you're indulging in a traditional Dutch meal or sampling dishes from around the world, Amsterdam's food scene is sure to satisfy your palate.

Before leaving Amsterdam Central, make sure to sample some Dutch cheese from a local shop or market. Also, consider booking a food tour to explore the city's culinary scene with a knowledgeable guide, or visiting a traditional Dutch restaurant to enjoy a hearty meal.

Amsterdam Centraal Station

Amsterdam Centraal Station is more than just a transportation hub; it's a symbol of the city's connectivity and a gateway to the rest of the Netherlands. The station's stunning Gothic and Renaissance Revival architecture is a sight to behold, making it one of Amsterdam's most iconic landmarks. As you arrive or depart from the station, take a moment to appreciate its architectural beauty and the hustle and bustle of daily life that surrounds it.

Inside the station, you'll find a wide range of facilities, including shops, restaurants, and a tourist information center. Whether you're catching a train to another city or simply exploring Amsterdam, the Centraal Station is a convenient and central starting point for your journey.

Before leaving Amsterdam Central, ensure you have a map of the city or a navigation app on your phone, as it can be easy to get lost in the winding streets of Amsterdam. Also, be aware that the station can be very busy, especially during rush hours, so plan your travels accordingly.

Final Thoughts

Amsterdam Central is the heart of the city, pulsating with energy and history. From the iconic Centraal Station to the delicious offerings of Dutch cuisine, this area of Amsterdam sets the tone for your adventure in this vibrant city. As you move on to explore other parts of Amsterdam, remember the practical tips shared in this chapter to make the most of your visit.

As you continue your journey through Amsterdam, let the city surprise you with its hidden gems and well-known landmarks. Explore the city with an open mind and a curious heart, and remember to respect the local customs and support local businesses.

Lastly, Amsterdam is a city that is best explored on foot or by bike, so make sure to pack comfortable shoes and consider renting a bike to explore the city like a local. And always keep an eye on your belongings, as pickpocketing can be common in busy areas.

With these practical tips in mind, you are ready to continue your journey through Amsterdam. Enjoy your adventure!

CHAPTER 2:
Historical Amsterdam

Amsterdam, often referred to as the "Venice of the North," is a city steeped in history. From its origins as a small fishing village in the 12th century to its growth into a major trading hub in the 17th century, Amsterdam's past is rich and varied. The city played a significant role in the Golden Age of the Netherlands, a period of great wealth and cultural achievement. Today, Amsterdam's historical heritage is evident in its well-preserved architecture, world-class museums, and vibrant neighborhoods. As you explore Historical Amsterdam, you will be transported back in time as you wander through narrow streets, cross picturesque canals, and visit historic buildings and museums. From the Amsterdam Museum, which tells the story of the city, to the Rembrandt House Museum, where the famous artist lived and worked, you will discover the history that shaped Amsterdam and made it the city it is today.

Before you start exploring Historical Amsterdam, it is recommended to plan your visit ahead of time. Many of the historical sites and museums are popular attractions and can get crowded, especially during peak tourist seasons. Consider purchasing tickets online in advance to avoid long lines and make the most of your time.

Amsterdam Museum

The Amsterdam Museum, formerly known as the Amsterdam Historical Museum, is a must-visit for anyone interested in the history of Amsterdam. Located in the former city orphanage, the museum offers a fascinating insight into the development of Amsterdam from the Middle Ages to the present day. The exhibitions cover a wide range of topics, from the city's origins as a small fishing village to its growth into a major trading hub and its role in the Golden Age of the Netherlands.

As you explore the museum, you will learn about the social, cultural, and economic changes that shaped Amsterdam over the centuries. You will discover the stories of the people who lived and worked in the city, and you will gain a deeper understanding of Amsterdam's history and its impact on the world.

Before visiting the Amsterdam Museum, it is advisable to check the museum's website for current exhibitions, opening hours, and any special events or guided tours that may be available during your visit. Also, consider combining your visit to the Amsterdam Museum with a walking tour of the surrounding area to get a more comprehensive understanding of the city's history.

Rembrandt House Museum

The Rembrandt House Museum, located in the house where the famous Dutch painter Rembrandt van Rijn lived and worked for almost 20 years, is another must-visit attraction for art and history enthusiasts. The museum is not only home to an impressive collection of Rembrandt's etchings, drawings, and paintings, but it also provides a glimpse into the artist's life and the 17th-century Amsterdam in which he lived.

As you tour the museum, you will see the artist's studio, where Rembrandt created many of his masterpieces, as well as the living quarters and the art collection he amassed during his lifetime. The museum also offers demonstrations on etching and paint preparation, providing insight into the techniques Rembrandt used to create his works.

Before visiting the Rembrandt House Museum, it is recommended to book your tickets online in advance, as the museum is a popular attraction and can get crowded. Also, consider taking a guided tour to gain a deeper understanding of Rembrandt's life and work, and to learn more about the history and significance of the museum's collection.

Begijnhof

The Begijnhof is one of Amsterdam's oldest inner courtyards and a true oasis of calm in the middle of the city. It was originally built in the 14th century as a residence for the Beguines, a lay Catholic sisterhood. Today, the Begijnhof is still inhabited by single women, and while the houses are private residences and not open to the public, visitors are welcome to enter the courtyard and enjoy its peaceful atmosphere.

As you stroll through the Begijnhof, you will be captivated by its historic charm. The courtyard is surrounded by well-preserved houses from the 17th and 18th centuries, and at its center stands the English Reformed Church, which dates back to the 15th century. There is also a hidden Catholic chapel in the Begijnhof, which serves as a reminder of the time when Catholicism was prohibited in Amsterdam.

Before visiting the Begijnhof, it is important to remember that it is a residential area, and visitors are asked to be respectful and keep noise levels to a minimum. Also, consider combining your visit to the Begijnhof with a walking tour of the surrounding area to learn more about the history and significance of this hidden gem.

The Old Church

The Old Church, or Oude Kerk, is Amsterdam's oldest building and a stunning example of Gothic architecture. Located in the heart of the Red Light District, it was consecrated in 1306 and has been a place of worship, a cultural center, and a historical monument over the centuries.

As you explore the Old Church, you will be struck by its grandeur and beauty. The church features a magnificent wooden ceiling, beautifully stained glass windows, and a historic organ that is one of the largest in the world. There are also several impressive works of art on display, including paintings by famous Dutch artists.

Before visiting the Old Church, it is advisable to check the church's website for current opening hours, admission fees, and any special events or concerts that may be taking place during your visit. Also, consider taking a guided tour to learn more about the history and significance of this important landmark.

The New Church

The New Church, or Nieuwe Kerk, is another important religious and historical landmark in Amsterdam. Located on Dam Square, next to the Royal Palace, the New Church was consecrated in 1409 and has been used for various purposes over the centuries, including royal coronations, weddings, and national ceremonies.

Today, the New Church is no longer used for religious services, but instead serves as an exhibition space for art, culture, and history. The church features a stunning interior with a beautifully carved pulpit, impressive organ, and intricate stained glass windows.

Before visiting the New Church, it is recommended to check the church's website for current exhibitions, opening hours, and admission fees. Also, consider combining your visit to the New Church with a tour of the Royal Palace, as the two landmarks are located next to each other and are significant to the history and culture of Amsterdam.

Westerkerk

The Westerkerk, or Western Church, is one of Amsterdam's most iconic landmarks. Located in the Jordaan neighborhood, it was built in the 17th century and is the largest Protestant church in the Netherlands. The church's tower, known as the Westertoren, is the tallest in Amsterdam and offers breathtaking views of the city.

As you explore the Westerkerk, you will be impressed by its stunning interior, which features a magnificent organ, beautifully carved wooden pulpit, and a series of impressive paintings. The church is also the final resting place of the famous Dutch painter Rembrandt van Rijn.

Before visiting the Westerkerk, it is advisable to check the church's website for current opening hours and any special events or concerts that may be taking place during your visit. Also, if you plan to climb the Westertoren, be prepared for a steep and narrow climb, but rest assured, the views from the top are well worth the effort.

The Jewish Quarter

The Jewish Quarter, or Jodenbuurt, is a historic neighborhood in Amsterdam that was once home to a thriving Jewish community. During World War II, the area was tragically decimated, and its Jewish population was deported. Today, the Jewish Quarter serves as a poignant reminder of the past and is home to several important landmarks, including the Jewish Historical Museum, the Portuguese Synagogue, and the Hollandsche Schouwburg.

As you explore the Jewish Quarter, take time to visit its various landmarks and learn about the history and significance of the area. The Jewish Historical Museum provides a comprehensive overview of Jewish life and culture in the Netherlands, while the Portuguese Synagogue, with its stunning interior and impressive collection of Torah scrolls, is a must-visit.

Before visiting the Jewish Quarter, it is recommended to plan your visit in advance, as some landmarks may have limited opening hours or require advance tickets. Also, consider taking a guided tour to gain a deeper understanding of the history and significance of the area.

Historic Canals

Amsterdam's historic canals, a UNESCO World Heritage Site, are an integral part of the city's identity and history. Constructed in the 17th century during the Dutch Golden Age, the canals were instrumental in the city's development as a major trading and cultural center.

As you explore the historic canals, you will be captivated by their beauty and charm. The canals are lined with picturesque canal houses, charming bridges, and vibrant houseboats, all of which contribute to the unique character of the city. Whether you choose to explore the canals by foot, bike, or boat, you will be rewarded with stunning views and photo opportunities.

Before exploring the historic canals, consider taking a guided canal cruise to learn more about the history and significance of the canals. Also, be sure to visit the Canal House Museum, which offers a fascinating insight into the history and architecture of the canal houses. And remember, the canals are not just a tourist attraction; they are a living, breathing part of Amsterdam's heritage, so be respectful and mindful as you explore.

Medieval Architecture

Amsterdam is renowned for its 17th-century canal ring, but the city also boasts some impressive medieval architecture. One of the most notable medieval structures is the Oude Kerk (Old Church), which is the oldest building in Amsterdam. Built in the 14th century, the Oude Kerk features stunning Gothic architecture, magnificent stained glass windows, and a wooden roof that is one of the largest medieval wooden vaults in Europe. Another remarkable medieval building is the De Waag, which was originally a city gate and later served as a weighing house. Today, it houses a restaurant and is one of the most iconic buildings in the city.

Before exploring Amsterdam's medieval architecture, it is advisable to do some research on the history and significance of the buildings you plan to visit. Also, consider taking a guided tour to gain a deeper understanding of the medieval architecture and its impact on the city's development. And remember, these historic buildings are not just tourist attractions; they are an integral part of Amsterdam's heritage, so be respectful and mindful as you explore.

Day Trip to Zaanse Schans

If you're interested in experiencing the Dutch countryside and stepping back in time to a bygone era, a day trip to Zaanse Schans is a must. Located just a short train ride from Amsterdam, Zaanse Schans is a historic village that offers a glimpse into the Netherlands' past. The village is home to a collection of well-preserved historic windmills, traditional Dutch houses, and artisan workshops.

As you explore Zaanse Schans, you will have the opportunity to visit working windmills, watch artisans at work, and learn about traditional Dutch crafts such as cheese making and clog carving. The village also offers stunning views of the surrounding countryside and is a great place for photography.

Before visiting Zaanse Schans, be sure to check the opening hours of the attractions you plan to visit, as some may have seasonal or limited hours. Also, consider taking a guided tour to learn more about the history and significance of the village and its attractions. And remember, Zaanse Schans is not just a tourist attraction; it is a living museum that preserves the heritage and traditions of the Netherlands, so be respectful and mindful as you explore.

Final Thoughts

As we conclude our exploration of historic Amsterdam, we hope that you have gained a deeper appreciation for the city's rich and varied past. From its medieval architecture to its iconic canals and historic landmarks, Amsterdam is a city steeped in history and tradition. Yet, it is also a city that is constantly evolving and embracing the future. This unique blend of old and new, tradition and innovation, is what makes Amsterdam so special.

As you continue your journey through Amsterdam, we encourage you to explore the city with a curious and open mind. Seek out the lesser-known landmarks and neighborhoods, engage with the locals, and immerse yourself in the city's vibrant culture. And remember, the history of Amsterdam is not just confined to museums and monuments; it is alive in the streets, the canals, and the people who call this city home.

Thank you for joining us on this journey through historic Amsterdam. We hope that it has been both informative and inspiring, and that it will serve as a foundation for your future explorations of this incredible city.

CHAPTER 3:
Artistic Amsterdam

Amsterdam's artistic heritage is as rich and varied as the city itself. Known for its world-class museums and vibrant art scene, this chapter delves into the heart of Artistic Amsterdam. From the masterpieces of the Dutch Golden Age to contemporary and modern art, the city offers a feast for the senses. As you wander through the art-filled streets, you'll discover why Amsterdam has long been a haven for artists, collectors, and art lovers. This journey will take you to iconic museums and hidden galleries, revealing the creative soul that pulsates through this remarkable city.

As you embark on your exploration of Artistic Amsterdam, remember to keep an open mind. Amsterdam's art scene is diverse, ranging from traditional to avant-garde, and each piece tells a unique story. Be prepared to be challenged, inspired, and moved by the art you encounter.

Stedelijk Museum

The Stedelijk Museum is a leading museum of modern and contemporary art and design in Amsterdam. As you step inside this iconic building, with its striking white façade and modernist design, you'll find yourself immersed in a world of artistic innovation and expression. The museum's extensive collection includes works by renowned artists such as Vincent van Gogh, Wassily Kandinsky, and Jackson Pollock, along with many others who have shaped and defined modern art.

As you wander through the galleries, take your time to appreciate the diverse range of artworks on display. From painting and sculpture to photography and graphic design, the Stedelijk Museum showcases a wide array of media and styles. The museum also regularly hosts temporary exhibitions, often focusing on contemporary artists and current themes in the art world.

To make the most of your visit to the Stedelijk Museum, consider joining a guided tour. These tours offer valuable insights into the collection and the stories behind the artworks. Also, check the museum's website in advance for information on current exhibitions and any special events that might be taking place during your visit.

MOCO Museum

The MOCO Museum, or Modern Contemporary Museum Amsterdam, offers a unique artistic experience, focusing on works by groundbreaking artists of the 20th and 21st centuries. Located in a beautiful townhouse overlooking Museumplein, the museum provides an intimate setting for exploring the works of artists such as Banksy, Andy Warhol, and Roy Lichtenstein.

The museum's collection includes a range of modern and contemporary art, with a particular emphasis on street art and pop art. As you explore the museum, you'll be struck by the vibrant colors, bold messages, and innovative techniques that characterize these artistic movements.

To enhance your visit to the MOCO Museum, consider using the audio guide available at the museum. It offers detailed commentary on the artworks and artists, enriching your understanding of the pieces on display. Additionally, since the museum is smaller and often busy, visiting during off-peak hours can provide a more relaxed and personal experience.

FOAM Photography Museum

The FOAM Photography Museum is a celebration of the photographic arts, nestled in the heart of Amsterdam. This museum showcases a broad spectrum of photography genres, from historical pictures to contemporary works, offering a platform for both world-renowned artists and emerging talents. As you step into FOAM, you'll find yourself in a space where photography is both an art form and a means of communication, telling stories that are captivating, thought-provoking, and deeply personal.

Each exhibition room in FOAM is designed to enhance the photographic experience, inviting you to engage with the images on a deeper level. Whether it's a powerful black and white portrait, a vibrant landscape, or an abstract photographic composition, each piece invites contemplation and dialogue.

To get the most out of your visit to FOAM, keep an eye out for special exhibitions and artist talks, which are regularly held at the museum. Photography enthusiasts may also want to explore the museum's extensive collection of photography books and prints. Visiting early in the morning or on weekdays can often provide a quieter and more intimate viewing experience.

The Eye Film Museum

The Eye Film Museum, strikingly located on the north bank of the IJ river, is a must-visit for film enthusiasts and those interested in cinematic arts. The museum's modern architecture is a visual treat, and its collections offer an insightful journey into the world of cinema. The museum houses an extensive archive of films, covering a wide range of genres, eras, and countries, along with temporary exhibitions that explore various aspects of filmmaking and film history.

As you explore the museum, you'll encounter a range of cinematic experiences - from classic movies to experimental film art. The museum also offers interactive exhibits, allowing visitors to delve into the technical aspects of filmmaking and the evolution of cinematic techniques.

For a truly memorable experience, catch a film in one of the museum's cinemas. The Eye Film Museum regularly screens a diverse selection of films, from early cinematic masterpieces to contemporary works. Also, the museum's restaurant and bar offer spectacular views of the IJ river and are perfect for a post-visit discussion or relaxation.

Art Galleries in Jordaan

The Jordaan district, with its picturesque canals and narrow streets, is not only a historic part of Amsterdam but also a thriving hub for contemporary art. The area is dotted with a myriad of art galleries, showcasing a diverse range of art forms, from traditional oil paintings to modern installations. Strolling through Jordaan, you'll find galleries tucked away in charming buildings, each offering a unique glimpse into the world of art.

As you wander from one gallery to another, take the opportunity to engage with gallery owners and artists. Many of these galleries in Jordaan are run by artists themselves, who are often happy to discuss their work and provide insights into the local art scene.

To fully immerse yourself in Jordaan's art scene, consider visiting during an opening night or a gallery weekend, when the area comes alive with art enthusiasts and collectors. Also, many galleries in Jordaan are small and intimate, offering a more personal viewing experience compared to larger museums.

Street Art in NDSM

NDSM, a former shipyard in Amsterdam Noord, has transformed into a vibrant canvas for street artists from around the world. This area, with its industrial backdrop, provides a unique setting for an array of colorful and dynamic street art. As you explore NDSM, you'll be treated to a visual feast of murals, graffiti, and installations that reflect the creativity and spirit of Amsterdam's street art community.

Walking through NDSM, each turn and corner presents a new piece of art, ranging from large-scale murals to subtle, intricate pieces. This outdoor gallery captures the essence of contemporary urban culture and is a testament to the ever-evolving art scene in Amsterdam.

To get the most out of your visit to NDSM, consider taking a guided street art tour. These tours are often led by local artists or street art enthusiasts who can provide insights into the artists' backgrounds and the stories behind the artworks. Also, NDSM is known for its artistic events and workshops, so check the local event calendar to see what's happening during your visit.

Amsterdam's Music Scene

Amsterdam's music scene is as diverse and lively as the city itself, spanning a wide range of genres and styles. From classical concerts in historic venues to live jazz in cozy cafés, and from electronic music festivals to intimate indie gigs, there's something for every music lover in Amsterdam.

The city's concert halls, such as the Royal Concertgebouw and Muziekgebouw aan 't IJ, host world-class performances throughout the year. For those interested in jazz and blues, the clubs and bars of Amsterdam offer nightly live performances. The vibrant electronic music scene is not to be missed either, with Amsterdam being home to some of the world's most renowned DJs and electronic music festivals.

For a comprehensive musical experience, check the schedule of performances at various venues before your visit. Also, consider exploring the city's smaller, lesser-known venues for unique and intimate musical experiences. Remember to book tickets in advance for popular concerts and festivals, as they can sell out quickly.

Contemporary Architecture

Amsterdam is not only about historic buildings and traditional Dutch architecture; the city also boasts impressive contemporary architecture that adds a modern twist to its skyline. The Eastern Docklands, IJburg, and Zuidas are some of the areas where modern architecture enthusiasts can find innovative designs and cutting-edge buildings.

As you explore these areas, you'll encounter a range of architectural styles, from sleek and minimalist to bold and futuristic. Notable buildings include the EYE Film Institute, the Amsterdam Public Library, and the NEMO Science Museum. These structures are not only visually striking but also represent Amsterdam's commitment to architectural innovation and sustainable design.

To appreciate Amsterdam's contemporary architecture, consider taking an architectural tour or renting a bike to explore these areas at your own pace. Many modern buildings in Amsterdam are also known for their sustainability features, so keep an eye out for green roofs, energy-efficient designs, and innovative uses of space.

Day Trip to Haarlem

Just a short train ride from Amsterdam, Haarlem offers an artistic journey into a city rich in history and culture. Known for its picturesque streets, historic architecture, and vibrant art scene, Haarlem is a perfect destination for a day trip. The city was a major center for Dutch painting in the Golden Age and is home to the Frans Hals Museum, dedicated to one of the most celebrated Dutch painters. Here, you can admire Hals' lively and innovative portraits, along with works by other artists of the era.

In addition to the Frans Hals Museum, Haarlem's charming streets and squares are dotted with galleries and artisan shops. The Grote Markt, the heart of Haarlem, surrounded by historic buildings, offers a picturesque setting for exploring the city's artistic offerings.

Before heading to Haarlem, plan your visit to coincide with any special exhibitions or art events. Haarlem is also known for its unique boutiques and antique shops, making it ideal for those interested in arts and crafts. Don't forget to stroll along the river Spaarne and enjoy the scenic views that have inspired countless artists.

Final Thoughts

As we conclude our exploration of Artistic Amsterdam, it's clear that the city's artistic heritage is deeply woven into its fabric. From the grand museums showcasing masterpieces of classical and modern art to the vibrant street art in NDSM and the eclectic music scene, Amsterdam is a city where art is not just observed but lived and breathed.

For those seeking more artistic adventures, the neighborhoods of Jordaan and De Pijp offer a wealth of galleries and studios showcasing contemporary works. The Spiegelkwartier is another area worth exploring, known for its antique shops and art dealers.

Remember to keep an eye out for the city's architectural gems as you wander through Amsterdam. The harmonious blend of historical and contemporary design is a visual reminder of the city's artistic evolution. In addition, many cafes and bars in Amsterdam are adorned with artworks, offering a casual setting to enjoy both art and local life.

Lastly, Amsterdam's art scene is ever-changing, with new exhibitions, performances, and installations continuously emerging. Each visit to this city can offer new artistic insights and experiences. So, whether you're an art aficionado or simply appreciate the beauty in everyday life, Amsterdam's artistic landscape is sure to inspire and captivate.

CHAPTER 4: MODERN AMSTERDAM 51

CHAPTER 4:
Modern Amsterdam

Modern Amsterdam is a city that boldly embraces the future while honoring its rich history. It's a place where cutting-edge design and innovative architecture coexist with centuries-old canals and historic buildings. This chapter will guide you through Amsterdam's modern marvels, showcasing the city's flair for creativity and its commitment to sustainability. From awe-inspiring viewpoints to interactive science experiences, Modern Amsterdam offers a glimpse into a world where tradition meets innovation. As you explore, you'll discover how the city's forward-thinking approach has shaped its landscape, culture, and lifestyle.

As you embark on your exploration of Modern Amsterdam, keep an open mind to the innovative concepts and designs you'll encounter. This part of the city is a testament to how contemporary ideas can harmoniously blend with historical context, creating a dynamic and vibrant urban environment.

A'DAM Lookout

The A'DAM Lookout is an iconic tower offering panoramic views of Amsterdam. Situated on the north bank of the IJ river, this modern marvel provides a unique perspective on the city. The tower's observation deck offers a 360-degree view, allowing you to take in the sprawling urban landscape, the historic city center, and the vast waterways that define Amsterdam.

In addition to the stunning views, the A'DAM Lookout is home to an interactive exhibition about Amsterdam's history and culture. For thrill-seekers, the tower offers 'Over The Edge,' Europe's highest swing, where you can swing out over the edge of the tower for an exhilarating experience.

Before visiting the A'DAM Lookout, consider booking your tickets in advance, especially for the swing, as it's a popular attraction. Also, visiting during sunset can provide a breathtaking experience as the city transitions from day to night. The tower is easily accessible by a short ferry ride from Central Station, adding to the adventure of your visit.

NEMO Science Museum

The NEMO Science Museum, with its distinctive ship-like architecture, is a celebration of science and technology. Located near Amsterdam Central Station, NEMO takes you on an interactive and educational journey through the world of science. The museum's hands-on exhibits are designed to engage visitors of all ages, making it a perfect destination for families or anyone with a curious mind.

Inside NEMO, you can explore topics ranging from biology and chemistry to physics and technology. The museum's rooftop offers not only spectacular views of the city but also an outdoor exhibition about sustainable living and renewable energy. To make the most of your visit to NEMO, allow plenty of time to explore all five floors of exhibits. The museum can be particularly busy on weekends and during school holidays, so consider visiting on a weekday for a more relaxed experience.

Also, don't miss the opportunity to participate in the science demonstrations and workshops that NEMO offers, providing a deeper understanding of scientific concepts in a fun and interactive way.

IJburg

IJburg, a group of artificial islands in the eastern part of Amsterdam, represents modern urban planning and architecture at its finest. This contemporary neighborhood stands as a testament to Amsterdam's innovative approach to city expansion and sustainable living. As you explore IJburg, you'll be struck by its modern residential buildings, creative use of space, and the integration of water in its design. The area offers a mix of residential, commercial, and recreational spaces, including beaches, marinas, and parks.

One of the highlights of IJburg is its architecture. Here, you'll find a variety of building styles, from minimalist and sleek to colorful and experimental. As you walk through the neighborhood, take time to appreciate the creativity and thought that have gone into designing these spaces.

When visiting IJburg, a walk along the IJburg Beach (Strand IJburg) is highly recommended. This urban beach offers a great spot for relaxation and enjoying views of the water. For architecture enthusiasts, consider taking a guided tour to learn more about the development and design of IJburg. The area is easily accessible by tram from the city center, making it a convenient destination for those looking to explore modern Amsterdam.

Amsterdam Noord

Amsterdam Noord, located across the IJ river from the city center, has transformed from an industrial area into one of the city's most creative and vibrant neighborhoods. This district is known for its innovative cultural spaces, artistic communities, and modern architecture. As you venture into Amsterdam Noord, you'll discover a mix of repurposed industrial buildings and contemporary architectural developments.

One of the must-visit spots in Amsterdam Noord is the NDSM Wharf, a former shipyard turned cultural hotspot. Here, you'll find a range of creative businesses, art studios, and trendy cafes. The area also hosts various cultural events and festivals throughout the year.

To experience the essence of Amsterdam Noord, consider renting a bike to explore the neighborhood's artistic murals and street art. The ferry ride from Central Station to Amsterdam Noord is an experience in itself, offering great views of the IJ river and the city skyline. Don't forget to visit the EYE Film Institute and the A'DAM Lookout, both located in Noord and offering unique cultural and visual experiences.

Amsterdam ArenA

The Amsterdam ArenA, home to the famous Ajax football team, is not only a sports venue but also an architectural landmark. Located in the southeast of Amsterdam, the stadium is known for its modern design and state-of-the-art facilities. Whether you're a football fan or not, a visit to the Amsterdam ArenA is an opportunity to experience the excitement and energy of one of Europe's most renowned stadiums.

For football enthusiasts, taking a guided tour of the Amsterdam ArenA is a must. The tour offers behind-the-scenes access to areas usually off-limits to the public, including the dressing rooms, the players' tunnel, and the pitch itself. You'll also learn about the history and achievements of Ajax Amsterdam.

If you plan to visit the Amsterdam ArenA, check the schedule for any matches or events taking place during your stay. Attending a live football match can be an exhilarating experience, immersing you in the local culture and passion for the sport. The stadium also hosts concerts and other events, so there might be something else exciting happening during your visit.

Modern Dutch Design

Amsterdam has long been a hub for modern Dutch design, known for its minimalist and functional aesthetics. This design philosophy is evident in various aspects of the city, from interior design and fashion to urban planning and public spaces. A visit to the Museum of Bags and Purses or the Droog design studio in the city center will give you a glimpse into the world of Dutch design.

One particular area to explore for design enthusiasts is the De Pijp neighborhood. Known for its trendy boutiques and concept stores, De Pijp is a showcase of contemporary Dutch design, offering everything from home decor to avant-garde fashion. The Hôtel Droog, located in the heart of Amsterdam, is another must-visit for design lovers. This one-room hotel is surrounded by a gallery, a design shop, and a beautiful garden, all embodying the essence of Dutch design.

When exploring Amsterdam's design scene, consider visiting during the annual Dutch Design Week, which offers a series of events, workshops, and exhibitions throughout the city. Also, many cafes and restaurants in Amsterdam feature interiors designed by leading Dutch designers, providing an opportunity to experience modern design in everyday settings.

Technology and Innovation

Amsterdam is a city at the forefront of technology and innovation, with a focus on smart city solutions and digital innovation. The Amsterdam Smart City initiative, for example, is transforming the way the city operates, from energy consumption to traffic management. A visit to the Marineterrein Amsterdam, a former naval base turned innovation district, offers insights into cutting-edge research and technology development happening in the city.

The Science Park Amsterdam, home to research institutes, startups, and the University of Amsterdam's Faculty of Science, is another hub for innovation and technology. Here, you can explore the latest advancements in science and technology and see how they are being applied to solve real-world problems.

To experience Amsterdam's commitment to technology and innovation, consider visiting during one of the city's tech festivals or conferences, such as The Next Web Conference. Additionally, many coworking spaces and innovation labs in Amsterdam offer tours and events that are open to the public, providing a closer look at the city's vibrant startup ecosystem.

Sustainable Amsterdam

Sustainability is a key focus in Amsterdam, with the city aiming to become one of the most sustainable urban centers in the world. This commitment is evident in various initiatives, from green energy and sustainable transportation to eco-friendly buildings and waste management. The Zuidas district, known as Amsterdam's financial center, is also home to some of the most sustainable office buildings in the Netherlands.

The city's efforts in promoting cycling as a primary mode of transportation is a testament to its dedication to sustainability. Exploring Amsterdam by bike not only gives you an authentic local experience but also contributes to the city's eco-friendly ethos. Additionally, the city's parks, such as the Amsterdamse Bos and Vondelpark, offer green spaces for relaxation and recreation, further enhancing its sustainable lifestyle.

Visitors interested in sustainable living can explore the De Ceuvel in Amsterdam Noord, a sustainable planned workspace for creative and social enterprises. This unique space is built on a former shipyard and features upcycled houseboats set on land. For those looking to stay in eco-friendly accommodations, Amsterdam offers a range of sustainable hotels and hostels focused on minimizing their environmental impact.

Day Trip to Rotterdam

A day trip to Rotterdam, just an hour away by train from Amsterdam, offers a stark contrast with its modern and innovative architecture. Known for its cutting-edge design, Rotterdam was rebuilt after being heavily bombed in World War II and has since embraced modernity and innovation. The city's skyline, marked by futuristic skyscrapers, is a testament to its architectural daring. Key sites include the Cube Houses, the Erasmus Bridge, and the Markthal, a stunning indoor market and residential building.

In Rotterdam, sustainability and modern urban planning are evident. The city has implemented various green initiatives, making it a leading example of sustainable urban development. A visit to the DakAkker, one of Europe's largest rooftop farms, showcases innovative urban farming techniques. Rotterdam's commitment to green spaces, sustainable living, and modern architecture makes it a fascinating complement to your exploration of modern Amsterdam.

Final Thoughts

Exploring Modern Amsterdam offers a glimpse into a city that seamlessly integrates its historical charm with a forward-looking approach to urban living. This chapter has taken you through the innovative landmarks, sustainable practices, and creative spaces that define the city's modern character. From the panoramic views at the A'DAM Lookout to the technological wonders of NEMO Science Museum, and the eco-conscious design in IJburg, Amsterdam is a city where the future is being shaped today.

As you continue to discover Amsterdam, take time to explore areas like the Zuidas district, known for its modern architecture and dynamic business environment, and the Houthavens, a former industrial area transformed into a sustainable living and working space. These areas offer a deeper understanding of how Amsterdam is evolving and adapting to the challenges of the 21st century.

Remember, the essence of Modern Amsterdam lies not only in its physical structures but in its spirit of innovation and sustainability. Whether you're marveling at the latest architectural marvel, enjoying the greenery of an urban park, or experiencing the city's progressive art scene, Amsterdam invites you to consider the possibilities of modern urban living. As you depart from this chapter, carry with you the inspiration and insights gained from a city that looks to the future while honoring its past.

CHAPTER 5:
Amsterdam Cuisine

Amsterdam's culinary scene is a delightful reflection of its cultural diversity and rich history. In this chapter, we will embark on a gastronomic journey through Amsterdam, exploring the traditional flavors and contemporary culinary innovations that make the city's cuisine unique. From classic Dutch dishes to international fusion, Amsterdam offers a palate-pleasing experience for every kind of food lover. As you explore the city's eateries, from cozy cafés to high-end restaurants, you will discover how Amsterdam blends local ingredients with global influences to create a dining experience that is both authentic and innovative.

As you savor the flavors of Amsterdam, remember to explore beyond the tourist hotspots. The city's culinary scene is vibrant and varied, with hidden gems waiting to be discovered in its many neighborhoods. Whether you're indulging in street food or dining in a Michelin-starred restaurant, Amsterdam's cuisine is sure to delight your taste buds.

Dutch Cheese

No culinary exploration of Amsterdam would be complete without tasting its world-famous Dutch cheese. The Netherlands is renowned for its cheese-making tradition, and Amsterdam offers ample opportunities to sample a wide variety of Dutch cheeses, such as Gouda, Edam, and Leyden. Cheese shops and markets throughout the city provide a chance to taste and learn about the different flavors and aging processes.

One of the best ways to experience Dutch cheese is by visiting a traditional cheese market or one of the many specialty cheese shops in Amsterdam. These shops often offer cheese-tasting sessions, where you can sample a selection of cheeses paired with wines or local beers.

For a truly authentic experience, consider visiting the Amsterdam Cheese Museum or taking a cheese-tasting tour. These experiences not only allow you to taste a variety of cheeses but also provide insights into the history and culture of Dutch cheese-making. Remember to ask about pairing suggestions to enhance your cheese-tasting experience.

Bitterballen

Bitterballen, a quintessential Dutch snack, are a must-try for anyone visiting Amsterdam. These deep-fried, crispy balls are filled with a savory mixture of meat (usually beef or veal), broth, butter, flour, and spices. Bitterballen are typically served with mustard for dipping and are a popular accompaniment to a cold beer.

You'll find bitterballen on the menu at most bars and pubs in Amsterdam, making them a perfect snack to enjoy while experiencing the city's vibrant nightlife. They are also a staple at Dutch parties and gatherings.

To enjoy bitterballen like a local, head to a traditional 'brown café' – these are old Dutch pubs known for their cozy atmosphere and hearty fare. Bitterballen are best enjoyed hot and fresh, so order them with a local beer for a truly authentic Dutch experience. Keep in mind that they are usually served piping hot, so take care when biting into them!

Stroopwafels

Stroopwafels are one of Amsterdam's sweetest delights. These thin, round waffles filled with a rich caramel-like syrup are a traditional Dutch treat that have gained popularity worldwide. Originally from the city of Gouda, stroopwafels have become a staple in Amsterdam's cafes and bakeries. Freshly made stroopwafels, warm and gooey, are particularly irresistible.

You'll find stroopwafels at street markets, specialty shops, and even in supermarkets. However, for the freshest experience, head to a local market where they are made right before your eyes. The Albert Cuyp Market and the Lindenmarkt are great places to find vendors offering these delicious treats.

When indulging in a stroopwafel, pair it with a cup of Dutch coffee or tea for a delightful snack. For a unique twist, some cafes in Amsterdam offer stroopwafel-flavored ice cream, cakes, and even liqueurs. Don't forget to take a pack of stroopwafels home with you – they make great gifts for friends and family.

Seafood

Amsterdam's location near the North Sea means that seafood is a prominent feature of the city's cuisine. The Dutch have a long history of fishing, and this is reflected in the quality and variety of seafood available in Amsterdam. From herring, a national delicacy typically eaten raw with onions, to kibbeling (battered and fried fish pieces), Amsterdam's seafood is fresh and flavorful.

For a taste of traditional Dutch seafood, visit a haringhandel (herring cart) where you can try haring in the classic Dutch way. Seafood restaurants and fish markets in Amsterdam also offer a wide range of seafood options, from mussels and oysters to salmon and shrimp. Seafood lovers should consider visiting during the Hollandse Nieuwe (Dutch New Herring) season, which starts in mid-June when the first catch of the season is celebrated. Additionally, a visit to a local fish market, like the Fish Center at Albert Cuyp Market, can be a delightful culinary adventure.

Pancakes and Poffertjes

Pancakes and poffertjes are two delightful treats that are beloved in Amsterdam and throughout the Netherlands. Dutch pancakes, known as pannekoeken, are larger and thinner than the American version and can be enjoyed with a variety of sweet and savory toppings. Poffertjes, on the other hand, are small, fluffy pancakes, typically served with powdered sugar and butter.

You can find these delectable treats at pancake houses and street markets throughout the city. Poffertjes are particularly popular at festivals and outdoor events, where they are often made fresh on large, specialized griddles.

For a memorable pancake experience, visit one of Amsterdam's traditional pancake houses where you can enjoy a wide range of flavors and toppings. Some restaurants even offer innovative takes on these classic dishes, incorporating international ingredients and flavors. Don't miss the opportunity to try poffertjes as a sweet snack while exploring Amsterdam – they are a delight for both adults and children alike.

Dutch Beer and Jenever

The Dutch brewing tradition is an integral part of Amsterdam's culinary landscape, with an impressive array of local beers and the traditional Dutch spirit, jenever. Amsterdam is home to numerous breweries, ranging from historic establishments to modern craft breweries, each offering a unique selection of beers. A visit to one of these breweries often includes a tour and a tasting session, providing insights into the brewing process and the chance to sample various beer styles.

Jenever, often referred to as Dutch gin, is another traditional beverage worth exploring. It's a juniper-flavored spirit that comes in two main varieties: oude (old) and jonge (young), which refer to the production style rather than the age. Jenever tastings can be found in traditional Dutch bars, known as 'brown cafes,' and at distilleries throughout the city.

For those interested in exploring Dutch beer and jenever, consider visiting a local brewery or distillery for a guided tour and tasting. Additionally, many bars in Amsterdam offer a wide selection of local and craft beers, making them perfect places to relax and enjoy the city's brewing culture. Remember to drink responsibly and immerse yourself in the rich history and flavors of these traditional Dutch beverages.

Food Markets

Amsterdam's food markets are a culinary adventure, offering a taste of local and international cuisines. These markets, found throughout the city, are a great way to experience Amsterdam's vibrant food scene. The Albert Cuyp Market, one of the largest and most popular street markets in Europe, offers a variety of fresh produce, cheeses, fish, spices, and street food. Another notable market is the Noordermarkt, which hosts a weekly organic farmer's market.

Exploring these markets provides an opportunity to sample a variety of foods, interact with local vendors, and purchase fresh ingredients. The markets are also perfect for picking up picnic supplies before heading to one of Amsterdam's beautiful parks. For a true taste of local culture, plan your market visit around lunchtime when the food stalls are bustling with activity. Many markets also offer local delicacies that are hard to find elsewhere, making them a must-visit for foodies. Don't forget to bring cash, as not all vendors accept credit cards.

Cooking Classes

For those who want to delve deeper into Dutch cuisine, participating in a cooking class is an excellent way to learn about local cooking techniques and recipes. Amsterdam offers a variety of cooking classes, ranging from traditional Dutch cooking to international cuisines. These classes provide a hands-on experience, often including a visit to a local market to select fresh ingredients.

Cooking classes in Amsterdam cater to all skill levels, whether you're a seasoned cook or a beginner. They provide an opportunity not only to learn new cooking skills but also to understand the cultural significance of the dishes you prepare.

When selecting a cooking class, consider one that focuses on seasonal and locally sourced ingredients to get a true taste of Dutch cuisine. These classes are not just about learning to cook; they're about experiencing the joy of creating and sharing a meal. Additionally, cooking classes can be a great way to meet locals and fellow travelers, making them a memorable part of your Amsterdam experience.

Traditional Dutch Dishes

Exploring Amsterdam's culinary scene would not be complete without trying some traditional Dutch dishes. These hearty and comforting meals reflect the country's history and cultural influences. 'Stamppot,' a dish of mashed potatoes mixed with vegetables like kale, carrots, or sauerkraut, often served with smoked sausage, is a staple during the colder months. Another classic is 'Erwtensoep,' a thick pea soup with pork and sausage, perfect for a winter day.

For those with a sweet tooth, 'Appeltaart' (Dutch apple pie) is a must-try. This deep-dish pie, filled with apples and spices and often served with whipped cream, can be found in cafes and bakeries throughout the city. Another sweet treat is 'Ontbijtkoek,' a spiced cake typically enjoyed with a smear of butter alongside coffee or tea.

To experience these traditional dishes, head to a local 'eetcafé' (a casual restaurant) or a traditional Dutch restaurant. Many places in the Jordaan and De Pijp neighborhoods offer an authentic Dutch dining experience. Don't hesitate to ask locals for their favorite spots – they'll likely be happy to share their recommendations.

Dining Etiquette in Amsterdam

Understanding dining etiquette in Amsterdam can enhance your culinary experience. Dutch dining is generally informal, but politeness and respect are always appreciated. It's common to greet the staff when entering and leaving a restaurant. Tipping is customary in Amsterdam; while service is usually included in the bill, it's polite to leave a small tip (around 5-10%) for good service.

In Amsterdam, dinner is typically the main meal of the day, usually eaten around 6-8 PM. It's a good idea to make a reservation for dinner, especially at popular restaurants. When dining out, take your time to enjoy your meal – the Dutch appreciate a relaxed dining atmosphere. For a unique dining experience, explore the city's diverse neighborhoods. Each area offers its own culinary specialties, from Indonesian cuisine in De Pijp to seafood restaurants along the canals. Street food vendors and food trucks are also great for a quick and tasty bite.

Final Thoughts

Amsterdam's cuisine is as diverse and intriguing as the city itself, offering a blend of traditional flavors and contemporary culinary innovation. From hearty Dutch staples to international delights, the city caters to a variety of palates and dining preferences.

As you explore Amsterdam, consider visiting the vibrant Foodhallen in Oud-West, an indoor food market where you can sample a range of cuisines. For a more upscale dining experience, the Michelin-starred restaurants in the Museum Quarter offer exquisite dishes in elegant settings.

Remember, Amsterdam's culinary scene extends beyond its restaurants and cafes. The city's markets, food festivals, and cooking classes offer immersive culinary experiences that provide insight into the local culture and cuisine.

In conclusion, whether you're sampling street food by the canals or enjoying a fine dining experience, Amsterdam's culinary landscape is sure to leave a lasting impression. Enjoy the flavors of the city, and don't be afraid to try something new – you might just discover your new favorite dish.

AMSTERDAM TRAVEL GUIDE

CHAPTER 6: SHOPPING IN AMSTERDAM   75

CHAPTER 6:
Shopping in Amsterdam

Shopping in Amsterdam offers a delightful mix of traditional charm and contemporary trends. The city is renowned for its eclectic shopping experiences, ranging from bustling flea markets brimming with antiques and curiosities to chic fashion boutiques featuring the latest trends. This chapter will guide you through Amsterdam's diverse shopping landscape, where each district has its own unique character and offerings. Whether you're a bargain hunter, a fashion enthusiast, or simply looking for unique souvenirs, Amsterdam's shopping scene is sure to captivate and inspire you.

As you explore the shopping havens of Amsterdam, immerse yourself in the local culture and discover the creativity and craftsmanship that the city is known for. Remember, shopping in Amsterdam is not just about the items you purchase; it's about the experience and the stories behind them.

Flea Markets

Amsterdam's flea markets are treasure troves for those who love to hunt for vintage items, antiques, and unique finds. The Waterlooplein Market, one of the city's oldest and most famous flea markets, offers a wide range of goods, from clothes and accessories to books and vinyl records. Another notable market is the

IJ-Hallen, known as one of the largest flea markets in Europe, located in Amsterdam Noord.

Strolling through these markets, you'll find an eclectic mix of items, each with its own history and charm. Flea markets in Amsterdam are not only great for shopping but also for experiencing the local culture and mingling with the city's residents.

Before visiting the flea markets, it's a good idea to arrive early for the best selection of items. Bring cash, as many vendors don't accept cards, and be prepared to haggle – it's part of the fun and expected at flea markets. Also, check the opening days and times, as some markets are only open on specific days of the week.

Fashion Boutiques

For those interested in fashion, Amsterdam's boutique scene offers a range of styles, from high-end designer wear to independent labels and sustainable fashion. The Nine Streets (De Negen Straatjes) area, nestled within the city's historic canal belt, is home to numerous boutiques selling clothing, jewelry, and accessories. Each boutique in this area has its own unique style and often features local designers.

Another destination for fashion lovers is the Utrechtsestraat, known for its stylish clothing stores and specialty shops. Here, you can find contemporary Dutch designs and international brands, catering to a variety of tastes and budgets.

When shopping in Amsterdam's fashion boutiques, take the time to talk to the shop owners and staff. They often have a passion for fashion and can provide valuable insights into the latest trends and local designers. Additionally, many boutiques in Amsterdam are focusing on sustainable and ethical fashion, offering you a chance to make conscious choices while keeping up with style.

Bookshops

Amsterdam's bookshops are a haven for bibliophiles, offering an impressive selection of both Dutch and international literature. The city is home to several iconic bookstores, each with its unique charm and collection. The renowned American Book Center, located in the heart of Amsterdam, is known for its extensive selection of English-language books and its spiral staircase lined with books. Another gem is Boekhandel Van Rossum, a cozy store with a carefully curated collection and knowledgeable staff.

For those interested in rare and antique books, Amsterdam offers several specialized shops. Antiquariaat Brinkman, for instance, is a must-visit for collectors, offering a wide range of old and rare books.

When exploring Amsterdam's bookshops, set aside enough time to browse through their collections and enjoy the unique atmosphere each store offers. Many bookshops in Amsterdam also host readings, signings, and other literary events, providing an opportunity to engage with the local literary community. Don't forget to check out the smaller, independent bookshops scattered throughout the city for unique finds and local publications.

De Bijenkorf

De Bijenkorf, Amsterdam's premier luxury department store, offers a lavish shopping experience in a historic building on Dam Square. Known for its high-end brands and designer collections, De Bijenkorf caters to those looking for luxury fashion, beauty products, accessories, and home decor. The store's stunning architecture and elegant interior add to the luxurious atmosphere.

Apart from shopping, De Bijenkorf also features a gourmet food hall where shoppers can indulge in a variety of culinary delights, from classic Dutch treats to international cuisine. The rooftop terrace offers a splendid view of the city, making it a perfect spot to relax after shopping.

For an enhanced shopping experience at De Bijenkorf, consider taking advantage of their personal shopping service. Also, keep an eye out for the store's seasonal sales and special events, which offer opportunities to shop for high-end brands at discounted prices. Remember, even if you're not planning to make a purchase, De Bijenkorf is worth a visit for its architectural beauty and the wide range of high-quality products on display.

The Nine Streets

The Nine Streets (De Negen Straatjes) area is a picturesque shopping district in Amsterdam, known for its narrow streets and charming 17th-century architecture. This neighborhood is a hub for independent boutiques, artisanal shops, and vintage stores, offering a diverse shopping experience. Here, you can find everything from handmade jewelry and unique fashion to vintage furniture and Dutch design.

As you stroll through The Nine Streets, take the time to explore the side streets and alleyways – they often hide some of the area's most interesting shops. The district is also home to several cozy cafes and restaurants, making it a perfect spot for a shopping break. To make the most of your visit to The Nine Streets, consider exploring the area on foot or by bike, as this allows you to fully appreciate its quaint charm and discover hidden gems. Many shops in The Nine Streets are locally owned and offer products that are unique to Amsterdam, making them ideal for finding special gifts or souvenirs.

Antique Shops

Amsterdam's antique shops are a treasure trove for collectors and history enthusiasts. Nestled within the city's historic neighborhoods, these shops offer a wide range of antiques, from Dutch Golden Age paintings to Art Deco furniture and vintage jewelry. The Spiegelkwartier, a neighborhood near the Rijksmuseum, is particularly renowned for its high concentration of antique shops and galleries, making it a must-visit destination for antique lovers.

Each shop in the Spiegelkwartier has its own specialization, providing an opportunity to discover unique pieces and learn about different periods and styles. The knowledgeable shop owners are often passionate about their collections and happy to share stories and information about their items.

When exploring Amsterdam's antique shops, take your time to appreciate the craftsmanship and history of the items. It's also a good idea to inquire about the provenance of pieces you're interested in. For those who are serious about purchasing antiques, consider researching in advance and possibly consulting with an expert or appraiser. Remember, antique shopping in Amsterdam is not just about the purchase; it's about the experience and the stories behind the objects.

Dutch Design Stores

Dutch design, known for its innovation, functionality, and aesthetic appeal, is celebrated in numerous design stores across Amsterdam. These stores showcase a range of products, from furniture and lighting to homewares and fashion, all embodying the principles of Dutch design. Areas like the Jordaan and De Pijp are home to many of these design stores, offering a diverse selection of items created by both established designers and emerging talents.

Stores such as Droog in the city center and The Frozen Fountain in the Prinsengracht area are popular destinations for design enthusiasts. These stores not only sell products but also provide a glimpse into the latest trends in Dutch design.

When visiting Dutch design stores, consider looking for items that combine aesthetic beauty with practical functionality, a hallmark of Dutch design. Many stores also focus on sustainability, offering products made with eco-friendly materials and processes. Don't hesitate to ask store staff about the designers and the stories behind the products – it can add an extra layer of appreciation to your shopping experience.

Souvenir Shopping

Souvenir shopping in Amsterdam offers a chance to bring home a piece of the city's culture and heritage. From classic

Dutch souvenirs like wooden clogs, Delftware pottery, and tulip bulbs to more contemporary items like local artisanal products and Dutch design pieces, there's a wide range of options to choose from.

For traditional Dutch souvenirs, the souvenir shops in the city center near Dam Square and along the Kalverstraat are convenient options. However, for more unique and authentic souvenirs, exploring the city's markets and local boutiques can be more rewarding. The Albert Cuyp Market and the Flower Market are great places to find a variety of souvenirs, including food items like Dutch cheese and stroopwafels.

When shopping for souvenirs, consider supporting local artisans and small businesses. This not only provides you with a more authentic souvenir but also contributes to the local economy. Also, be mindful of the quality and origin of the items you purchase, especially when buying traditional crafts and artisan products.

Day Trip to Batavia Stad

For a unique shopping experience outside of Amsterdam, consider a day trip to Batavia Stad Fashion Outlet. Located about an hour's drive from Amsterdam, this outlet mall offers a variety of high-end brands and designer labels at discounted prices. With over 150 stores, Batavia Stad provides a comprehensive shopping experience, from luxury fashion and sportswear to lifestyle and home decor products.

Batavia Stad's picturesque setting, reminiscent of a 17th-century Dutch village, enhances the shopping experience. The outlet also offers a range of dining options, making it easy to spend a full day exploring and shopping.

Before heading to Batavia Stad, check the outlet's website for any special promotions or seasonal sales. Also, consider using the shuttle service offered from Amsterdam, which provides a convenient and hassle-free way to reach the outlet. Shopping at Batavia Stad is not only a great way to find deals on top brands but also a chance to explore a different part of the Netherlands.

Final Thoughts

Amsterdam's shopping scene offers a delightful mix of traditional charm and modern trends, catering to a wide range of tastes and preferences. From browsing through antique shops in the Spiegelkwartier and exploring Dutch design stores to finding unique souvenirs in local markets, shopping in Amsterdam is an experience in itself.

As you explore the city's shopping offerings, consider venturing into neighborhoods like Haarlemmerstraat and Utrechtsestraat, known for their eclectic mix of shops and boutiques. These areas provide a more local and less touristy shopping experience, with a variety of unique and independent stores.

Remember, shopping in Amsterdam is not just about the items you buy; it's about the experiences you have and the memories you create. Take the time to chat with shop owners and learn about the stories behind their products. Whether you're looking for fashion, art, antiques, or souvenirs, Amsterdam's diverse shopping scene is sure to provide something that catches your eye and captures the essence of this vibrant city.

AMSTERDAM TRAVEL GUIDE

CHAPTER 7:
Nightlife in Amsterdam

Amsterdam's nightlife is as diverse and vibrant as the city itself, offering something for every taste and style. From cozy traditional pubs to lively jazz clubs and cutting-edge nightclubs, the city comes alive after dark with a multitude of options for entertainment. In this chapter, we'll explore the various facets of Amsterdam's nightlife, taking you through historic brown cafés, renowned jazz venues, and more. Whether you're looking for a relaxed evening with friends or an all-night dance party, Amsterdam's nightlife scene promises an unforgettable experience.

As you delve into the nightlife of Amsterdam, remember to respect the city's residential areas and maintain a courteous attitude towards locals. Amsterdam's nightlife is not only about enjoyment but also about experiencing the city's culture and social life.

Brown Cafés

Brown cafés, named for their wood-paneled walls and cozy, time-worn interiors, are quintessentially Amsterdam. These traditional Dutch pubs offer a warm and inviting atmosphere, perfect for enjoying a local beer or jenever. Brown cafés are often steeped in history, with some dating back several centuries, providing a glimpse into the city's past.

In a typical brown café, you'll find a range of Dutch beers on tap, along with simple but delicious pub fare. These cafés are popular gathering spots for locals and are an ideal place to strike up a conversation with Amsterdammers. The Jordaan neighborhood is particularly known for its authentic brown cafés, each with its own character and charm.

To fully experience the brown café culture, consider visiting in the late afternoon or early evening when the atmosphere is most vibrant. Some notable brown cafés to visit include Café 't Smalle and Café Papeneiland, both known for their historic ambiance and excellent selection of drinks. Remember, these cafés are about more than just drinking; they are about soaking in the local culture and the laid-back Amsterdam way of life.

Jazz Clubs

Amsterdam has a rich jazz history and offers a variety of venues for live jazz music, ranging from intimate clubs to larger concert halls. These venues host performances by both local talents and international artists, covering a range of jazz styles from traditional to contemporary.

The Bimhuis, located near the Central Station, is one of Amsterdam's most famous jazz venues and offers spectacular views of the IJ river along with its music. Smaller jazz clubs like Jazz Café Alto in the Leidseplein area provide a more intimate setting, ideal for those who want to be up close to the musicians.

For jazz enthusiasts, it's advisable to check the performance schedules of these clubs in advance and book tickets or arrive early to secure a good spot. Many jazz clubs in Amsterdam also serve food and drinks, making them perfect for an evening of dining and entertainment. Exploring the jazz scene in Amsterdam is not only a musical journey but also an opportunity to connect with the city's artistic side.

Rooftop Bars

Rooftop bars in Amsterdam offer a unique way to experience the city's nightlife, combining stunning views with stylish settings. These venues are perfect for enjoying a drink while overlooking Amsterdam's picturesque skyline. From chic, modern terraces to more laid-back settings, each rooftop bar has its own vibe and charm.

A visit to SkyLounge Amsterdam, located atop the DoubleTree by Hilton Hotel near Centraal Station, offers panoramic views of the city. For a more relaxed atmosphere, Canvas on the 7th in the Volkshotel provides a great setting with its artistic vibe and often hosts DJs and live music events.

When planning a visit to a rooftop bar, it's advisable to check the weather forecast and dress accordingly, as evenings can be cooler. Making a reservation is also recommended, especially for popular spots. Rooftop bars in Amsterdam are not just about the drinks; they're about experiencing the city from a different perspective. Enjoy the ambiance, the views, and the company, making for a memorable Amsterdam night out.

Red Light District

The Red Light District, known locally as De Wallen, is one of Amsterdam's most famous areas for nightlife. Known for its neon-lit windows and adult entertainment, the district offers a unique experience that is part of the city's open-minded character. While it draws curiosity from visitors, it's important to approach this area with respect for the workers and the local regulations.

Beyond its famous windows, the Red Light District is also home to a variety of bars, clubs, and restaurants. The area's nightlife is vibrant and diverse, catering to a wide range of tastes. The district's history and unique atmosphere make it an interesting place to explore at night.

When visiting the Red Light District, remember to be respectful and discreet if you choose to explore this part of Amsterdam. Photography of the workers in the windows is strictly prohibited. Also, be aware of your surroundings and stay in well-lit, busy areas, especially late at night.

Nightclubs

Amsterdam's nightclub scene is renowned for its diversity and energy, offering everything from techno and house to hip-hop and indie music. The city's clubs are a testament to Amsterdam's status as one of the world's leading destinations for electronic music. Iconic clubs like Paradiso and Melkweg, both located in the Leidseplein area, are not only nightclubs but also concert venues, hosting a variety of music events and performances.

For techno and house music enthusiasts, clubs like De School and Warehouse Elementenstraat are must-visits. These venues are known for their cutting-edge sound systems and hosting world-renowned DJs.

Before planning a night out at Amsterdam's clubs, check the event schedules and consider purchasing tickets in advance, as popular events often sell out quickly. Be prepared for late nights, as many clubs in Amsterdam stay open until the early hours of the morning. Exploring Amsterdam's nightclub scene is an opportunity to experience the city's modern, energetic side and dance the night away to some of the best music in the world.

Cinema and Film

Amsterdam offers a rich cinema culture, ranging from mainstream blockbusters to independent films and documentaries. The city's cinemas, many of which are housed in beautifully preserved historic buildings, provide a unique viewing experience. The Tuschinski Theater, an Art Deco masterpiece located near Rembrandtplein, is one of the most stunning cinemas in Europe, combining a luxurious vintage interior with state-of-the-art technology.

For those interested in independent and international films, The Eye Film Museum in Amsterdam Noord is a must-visit. This modern building not only showcases a diverse range of films but also offers exhibitions on film history and culture. Another notable venue is the FilmHallen in Oud-West, known for its wide selection of indie films.

When planning a cinema outing in Amsterdam, consider checking the programming of various cinemas, as many offer special screenings, film festivals, and director Q&A sessions. Also, keep in mind that most foreign films are shown in their original language with Dutch subtitles, making them accessible to international visitors.

Live Music Venues

Amsterdam's live music scene is as diverse as the city itself, with venues hosting everything from rock and pop to jazz and classical music. For an intimate live music experience, venues like Bitterzoet and Paradiso Noord, Tolhuistuin offer performances by local and international artists in a cozy setting. Larger venues such as Ziggo Dome and AFAS Live host concerts by well-known bands and musicians.

Jazz enthusiasts will find a wealth of options, from the famous Bimhuis, a venue dedicated to jazz and improvised music, to smaller clubs like Bourbon Street, which offer live jazz on a nightly basis.

To make the most of Amsterdam's live music scene, check the schedules of various venues in advance, as popular concerts can sell out quickly. Exploring the city's live music venues is not only a chance to enjoy great performances but also to experience the local culture and meet new people.

Theatre and Performances

Amsterdam's theatre scene offers a wide range of performances, from traditional plays and avant-garde productions to dance and opera. The Royal Theater Carré, beautifully located along the Amstel River, is one of Amsterdam's most renowned venues, hosting a variety of shows including musicals, concerts, and circus performances.

The Stadsschouwburg, located at Leidseplein, is another major venue offering a range of Dutch and international productions. For those interested in contemporary and experimental theatre, Frascati and De Brakke Grond are excellent choices.

Many theatres in Amsterdam offer performances with English subtitles or are performed in English, making them accessible to international audiences. It's advisable to book tickets in advance, especially for popular shows. Attending a performance at one of Amsterdam's theaters is not only an evening of entertainment but also a way to immerse yourself in the city's rich artistic heritage.

Comedy Clubs

Amsterdam's comedy scene offers a variety of venues where you can enjoy a night of laughter and entertainment. From stand-up comedy and improv to cabaret and open-mic nights, the city's comedy clubs cater to all tastes. One of the most popular spots is Boom Chicago, located in the Jordaan neighborhood, known for its English-language improv and sketch comedy shows.

Other venues like Toomler, associated with the Comedytrain collective, feature performances by both local and international comedians. These clubs often have a cozy and intimate atmosphere, making for a great evening out where you can enjoy humor in a variety of styles.

When planning to visit a comedy club in Amsterdam, it's advisable to book tickets in advance, as shows can sell out quickly, especially on weekends. Many clubs also offer a bar or restaurant service, allowing you to enjoy a meal or drinks before or after the show. A night at a comedy club in Amsterdam is not just about the laughs; it's about experiencing the city's lively and diverse entertainment scene.

About "Don't Come to Amsterdam"

The "Don't Come to Amsterdam" campaign, launched by the city council, addresses the challenges posed by overtourism and its impact on the quality of life for residents. The campaign focuses on encouraging respectful behavior among visitors and discouraging the types of tourism that have contributed to disturbances in the city, particularly in areas like the Red Light District and entertainment zones.

The initiative emphasizes Amsterdam's rich cultural heritage, urging tourists to explore the city's museums, historical sites, and local neighborhoods while respecting the city's residents and environment. The campaign also targets specific demographics known for disruptive behavior, conveying a clear message that disrespectful tourists are not welcome in Amsterdam. As a visitor to Amsterdam, it's important to be mindful of this campaign and to respect the city, its residents, and its heritage. This means behaving responsibly, respecting local laws and customs, and being considerate of the impact your actions may have on the community.

Final Thoughts

Exploring the nightlife of Amsterdam is an adventure in itself, with the city offering a rich tapestry of experiences, from cozy brown cafés and vibrant jazz clubs to cutting-edge nightclubs and comedy venues. However, it's crucial to remember the importance of responsible tourism and respect for the city's residents.

As you enjoy Amsterdam's nightlife, consider venturing into less crowded areas and exploring the city's diverse neighborhoods, each offering its own unique nighttime ambiance. This approach not only helps to alleviate the pressure of overtourism but also enriches your experience of the city.

The "Don't Come to Amsterdam" campaign is a reminder of the delicate balance between enjoying the city's offerings and preserving its quality of life. By being a respectful and considerate visitor, you contribute to maintaining Amsterdam as a vibrant and welcoming destination for all.

CHAPTER 8:
Coffee Shops of Amsterdam

· ·

Amsterdam's coffee shops are renowned worldwide, known for their unique approach to cannabis and their contribution to the city's culture. In this chapter, we explore the world of Amsterdam's coffee shops, a significant yet often misunderstood part of the city's identity. These establishments, distinct from typical cafés, offer both locals and visitors a place to legally purchase and consume cannabis in a controlled and relaxed environment. As we delve into the coffee shop culture of Amsterdam, it's essential to approach this topic with an open mind and an understanding of local laws and customs.

When visiting Amsterdam's coffee shops, remember that they are a part of the city's culture and should be approached with respect and responsibility. This chapter aims to provide a deeper understanding of coffee shops, their history, and how to navigate them respectfully and enjoyably.

Coffee Shops vs. Cafés

In Amsterdam, it's important to distinguish between 'coffee shops' and 'cafés'. A 'coffee shop' in Amsterdam refers to an establishment where cannabis is sold and consumed, whereas a 'café' is a traditional establishment serving coffee, tea, pastries, and sometimes light meals. This distinction is crucial for visitors to understand to avoid confusion.

Cafés in Amsterdam offer a completely different atmosphere from coffee shops. They are ideal for those who want to enjoy a traditional Dutch coffee experience, perhaps along with a slice of appeltaart (apple pie) or a sandwich. Many cafés in Amsterdam boast charming interiors and are perfect for relaxing, reading, or watching the world go by.

When visiting Amsterdam, consider experiencing both types of establishments to fully appreciate the diverse culture of the city. Enjoy the lively and unique atmosphere of a coffee shop, but also take the time to unwind in the more laid-back setting of a traditional Dutch café.

History of Coffee Shops in Amsterdam

The history of coffee shops in Amsterdam dates back to the 1970s when the Dutch government decriminalized the possession of small amounts of cannabis. This led to the opening of the first coffee shops, which were initially informal establishments where people could purchase and consume cannabis. Over the years, these coffee shops have evolved into professional businesses, regulated by the government, and have become an integral part of Amsterdam's cultural landscape.

Coffee shops in Amsterdam played a significant role in shaping the city's liberal policies towards cannabis. They have also contributed to discussions on drug policy reform both in the Netherlands and internationally. The history of these establishments is a fascinating journey through the city's progressive approach to cannabis, balancing tolerance with regulation.

For those interested in the history of Amsterdam's coffee shops, some establishments display information and memorabilia that offer insights into their evolution. Additionally, visiting a few different coffee shops can give you a sense of the diversity and history of these unique Amsterdam institutions.

The Coffee Shop Experience

Visiting a coffee shop in Amsterdam offers a unique experience. These establishments range from cozy, laid-back venues to modern, stylish spaces, each with its own atmosphere and character. Coffee shops typically offer a menu of various cannabis strains, each with different effects and potency levels. Knowledgeable staff can provide advice on the selection, ensuring a safe and enjoyable experience for both novices and seasoned consumers.

In addition to cannabis, most coffee shops also offer a range of non-alcoholic beverages and light snacks. The ambiance in a coffee shop is usually relaxed and friendly, with an emphasis on providing a comfortable space for socializing and unwinding.

When visiting a coffee shop, it's important to start with small amounts, especially if you are not accustomed to cannabis. Always inquire about the strength and effects of different strains. Many coffee shops also provide board games, books, or music, contributing to a leisurely and enjoyable atmosphere. Remember, the goal of visiting a coffee shop is to relax and enjoy the experience in a responsible manner.

Popular Coffee Shops in Amsterdam

Amsterdam boasts a variety of coffee shops, each offering a unique experience. Some of the city's most popular coffee shops are known for their quality cannabis, distinctive ambiance, and friendly service. The Bulldog, one of Amsterdam's first coffee shops, has multiple locations and is known for its iconic status and vibrant atmosphere. Another notable spot is Barney's, praised for its high-quality strains and welcoming environment.

For those seeking a more local experience, coffee shops like Dampkring and Boerejongens offer a blend of quality products and authentic Amsterdam charm. These establishments are renowned for their knowledgeable staff and the quality of their cannabis.

When visiting popular coffee shops, be prepared for them to be busy, especially in tourist areas. Visiting during off-peak hours can provide a more relaxed experience. Also, many popular coffee shops are known not just for their cannabis but also for their design and décor, contributing to the overall experience.

Coffee Shop Etiquette

Understanding and adhering to coffee shop etiquette is crucial for a respectful and enjoyable visit. First and foremost, always respect the age restriction; you must be 18 years or older to enter a coffee shop. It's also important to note that most coffee shops have a 'no tobacco' policy, meaning you cannot smoke tobacco or mix it with cannabis inside the shop.

When purchasing cannabis, it's polite to buy a drink or a snack as well. This supports the coffee shop and enhances your experience. Be considerate of other guests and the staff, and maintain a calm and friendly demeanor.

Always consume responsibly. If you're unfamiliar with the effects of cannabis, seek advice from the staff and start with a small amount. Remember, the goal is to enjoy your time in a safe and respectful manner.

Edibles and Alternatives

In addition to smoking cannabis, many coffee shops in Amsterdam offer edibles, which are food products infused with cannabis. These can include baked goods like brownies and cookies, as well as candies and chocolates. Edibles provide an alternative way to consume cannabis, especially for those who prefer not to smoke.

When consuming edibles, it's important to be aware that the effects can be different from smoking. They often take longer to take effect and can be more potent and longer-lasting. It's advisable to start with a small amount and wait for at least an hour to feel the full effects before consuming more.

Some coffee shops also offer alternative products, such as CBD-infused items, which do not have psychoactive effects. These can be a good option for visitors who want to experience the coffee shop culture without the intoxicating effects of THC.

Coffee Shops in the Jordaan

The Jordaan district, known for its picturesque canals and historic buildings, is also home to some of Amsterdam's most beloved coffee shops. These establishments often blend seamlessly into the charming neighborhood, offering a more local and authentic experience compared to the more tourist-centric coffee shops in other parts of the city.

Coffee shops in the Jordaan tend to be smaller and more intimate, making them ideal for a relaxed and cozy cannabis experience. Many of these coffee shops have a loyal local clientele, which contributes to a friendly and welcoming atmosphere.

When exploring the Jordaan, take the time to stroll through its narrow streets and discover the unique coffee shops this area has to offer. Each has its own character and charm, reflecting the bohemian and artistic spirit of the Jordaan. Visiting these coffee shops can be a delightful way to experience a different side of Amsterdam's coffee shop culture.

Cannabis and Dutch Law

While cannabis is tolerated in Amsterdam's coffee shops, it's essential to understand the legal context. The Netherlands has a policy of decriminalization, meaning that while cannabis is not legal, its sale and use in small quantities are tolerated in licensed coffee shops. Possession of up to 5 grams for personal use is generally not prosecuted.

It's important to note that public consumption of cannabis outside of coffee shops is frowned upon and can lead to fines. Additionally, driving under the influence of cannabis is illegal and strictly enforced.

When purchasing cannabis in a coffee shop, be aware that there are limits to how much you can buy (usually no more than 5 grams per person per day). It's also illegal to take cannabis across international borders, even if traveling to another country where it's decriminalized. Understanding these laws and regulations ensures that you can enjoy Amsterdam's coffee shop culture responsibly and within the bounds of local laws.

Safety and Responsible Use

Safety and responsible use are paramount when visiting coffee shops in Amsterdam. While the city is known for its liberal policies towards cannabis, it's crucial for visitors to consume responsibly and be aware of their limits. This is especially important for those who are inexperienced with cannabis use.

When visiting a coffee shop, always start with small amounts and wait to understand the effects before consuming more. It's also advisable to avoid mixing cannabis with alcohol, as this can intensify the effects. Be aware of your surroundings, especially if you're unfamiliar with the city, and plan your return to your accommodation safely.

Keep in mind that while cannabis use is tolerated in designated areas, public consumption outside of coffee shops is generally not allowed and can lead to fines. Always be respectful of local residents and other visitors, and contribute to maintaining a safe and enjoyable environment for everyone.

Day Trip to Haarlem for Coffee Shop Culture

A day trip to Haarlem, a charming city close to Amsterdam, offers a different perspective on Dutch coffee shop culture. Haarlem's coffee shops are known for their laid-back atmosphere and are less crowded than those in Amsterdam, providing a more relaxed experience. The city itself, with its historic buildings and picturesque streets, adds to the charm of visiting its coffee shops.

In Haarlem, you can explore a variety of coffee shops, each with its own character. The city also offers cultural attractions like the Teylers Museum and the Grote Kerk, making it a well-rounded trip. Haarlem is easily accessible by train from Amsterdam, making it a convenient destination for those looking to explore beyond the capital.

Final Thoughts

Exploring Amsterdam's coffee shop culture offers an insight into one aspect of the city's unique and liberal character. However, it's important to remember the impact of tourism on local residents. The "Don't Come to Amsterdam" campaign highlights the need for respectful and responsible tourism, especially in areas like the Red Light District and coffee shop zones, which have faced issues with noise, littering, and public disturbances. As you enjoy Amsterdam's coffee shops, be mindful of your behavior and its impact on the city. Embrace the opportunity to learn about cannabis in a regulated and safe environment, but also explore the other rich cultural experiences Amsterdam has to offer. Remember, Amsterdam is much more than its coffee shops; it's a city with a vibrant history, stunning architecture, and a thriving arts scene. Responsible and respectful tourism will help ensure that Amsterdam remains a welcoming and beautiful city for both visitors and residents alike.

AMSTERDAM TRAVEL GUIDE

CHAPTER 9:
Off the Beaten Path
· ·

Amsterdam is a city of hidden gems and lesser-known locales that offer a refreshing escape from the well-trodden tourist paths. In this chapter, we delve into the quieter, more secluded parts of the city, where the essence of Amsterdam's charm and tranquility is palpable. From sprawling green spaces to vibrant local neighborhoods, these off-the-beaten-path destinations provide a deeper and more authentic experience of Amsterdam. They are perfect for those who wish to explore the city's lesser-known aspects and discover its secret treasures.

As you venture into these less crowded areas, you'll not only gain a more nuanced understanding of Amsterdam but also enjoy a more relaxed pace of exploration. Remember, these hidden corners of the city reveal the true heart of Amsterdam, away from the hustle and bustle of the main tourist attractions.

Amsterdamse Bos

The Amsterdamse Bos (Amsterdam Forest) is a vast park located on the outskirts of the city, offering a natural oasis of tranquility and beauty. This artificially created forest is three times the size of New York's Central Park and provides a plethora of outdoor activities. From picturesque walking and cycling paths to canoeing and horseback riding, the Amsterdamse Bos is a haven for nature lovers and outdoor enthusiasts.

The park also hosts several attractions, including the open-air theater, the Bosbaan rowing lake, and the Goat Farm Ridammerhoeve, where visitors can interact with farm animals and enjoy organic local produce. During the summer months, the forest comes alive with various festivals and outdoor events.

To make the most of your visit to the Amsterdamse Bos, consider renting a bike to explore its extensive network of paths. Check the park's event calendar to catch any special activities or performances. The forest is easily accessible by public transport or bike from the city center, making it an ideal destination for a day trip.

De Pijp

De Pijp, often referred to as Amsterdam's 'Latin Quarter,' is a vibrant and diverse neighborhood known for its bohemian atmosphere. This area, once a working-class district, is now filled with lively cafes, bars, restaurants, and boutiques. De Pijp is also home to the famous Albert Cuyp Market, the largest street market in the Netherlands, where you can find everything from fresh produce to clothes and accessories.

The neighborhood's narrow streets are lined with 19th-century architecture, adding to its charm. De Pijp is also known for its cultural diversity, reflected in the variety of international cuisines available in the area. From traditional Dutch eateries to Surinamese, Moroccan, and Turkish restaurants, the culinary options are endless.

Exploring De Pijp provides a glimpse into local Amsterdam life, away from the tourist crowds. Take the time to wander through its streets, relax in one of its many cafes, and absorb the lively yet laid-back atmosphere. De Pijp is also a great place to experience Amsterdam's nightlife, with many bars and clubs offering a more local experience.

Giethoorn

Giethoorn, often referred to as the "Venice of the North," is a picturesque village located in the province of Overijssel, a short trip from Amsterdam. Known for its quaint thatched-roof houses and a network of canals, Giethoorn offers a tranquil escape from the city's hustle and bustle. The village's charm lies in its car-free center, where transportation is mainly by water or on foot along its scenic paths.

Visitors can explore Giethoorn by renting a boat or joining a guided canal tour, providing a unique perspective of the village's beautiful homes and lush green landscapes. The experience is serene and almost fairytale-like, with the only sounds being the gentle splashes of oars and the birdsong.

To enjoy Giethoorn to its fullest, plan your visit on a weekday to avoid the crowds. Besides the canal tours, don't miss the opportunity to visit the local museums and galleries, which showcase the village's history and culture. Giethoorn is an ideal day trip destination for those looking to experience the peaceful side of the Dutch countryside.

Zuidoost

Amsterdam Zuidoost, or Southeast Amsterdam, is a culturally diverse and dynamic area of the city, often overlooked by tourists. This district offers a unique mix of urban culture, green spaces, and modern architecture. Zuidoost is home to a variety of cultural festivals and events, reflecting the multicultural community that resides there.

One of the highlights of Zuidoost is the Bijlmer Park, a large green space perfect for picnics, sports, and leisurely strolls. The area also boasts the Amsterdam ArenA, the home stadium of the Ajax football team, and the Ziggo Dome and AFAS Live, which host numerous concerts and events.

Exploring Zuidoost gives visitors a chance to experience a different side of Amsterdam, one that is vibrant and contemporary. The district's food markets and restaurants offer a range of international cuisines, showcasing the area's cultural diversity. When visiting Zuidoost, be open to new experiences and enjoy the unique blend of cultures and communities.

Het Schip

Het Schip, located in the Spaarndammerbuurt district, is an iconic example of the Amsterdam School of architecture. This building, designed by architect Michel de Klerk, is known for its expressive and organic form, resembling the shape of a ship. Today, Het Schip serves as a museum dedicated to the Amsterdam School, offering insights into this influential architectural style.

The museum provides guided tours, showcasing the building's intricate brickwork, unique design elements, and the history of social housing in Amsterdam. The surrounding neighborhood also features other notable examples of Amsterdam School architecture, making it a fascinating area to explore for architecture enthusiasts.

Visiting Het Schip and the Spaarndammerbuurt area allows for a deeper appreciation of Amsterdam's architectural heritage. The museum is not only a journey through the history of architecture but also a testament to the city's commitment to innovative and aesthetic social housing solutions. Remember to check the museum's opening hours and tour schedules before your visit.

Hidden Courtyards

Amsterdam's hidden courtyards, or 'hofjes', are serene oases tucked away behind bustling streets and canals, offering a glimpse into the city's tranquil side. These historic courtyards, often dating back to the 17th and 18th centuries, were originally built as almshouses for the elderly and are characterized by their beautiful gardens and traditional Dutch architecture.

The Begijnhof is one of the most famous courtyards, known for its peaceful atmosphere and historic houses. Another notable hofje is the Claes Claesz Hofje, located in the Jordaan district, which features charming houses surrounding a well-kept garden. Exploring these hidden courtyards allows for a peaceful retreat from the city's busy pace.

When visiting these courtyards, remember to respect the privacy of the residents, as many of these hofjes are still inhabited. These tranquil spots are perfect for quiet contemplation and enjoying a moment of serenity amidst the city's hustle and bustle. The courtyards can often be easily missed, so keep an eye out for small archways and doors that lead into these hidden gems.

Unusual Museums

Amsterdam is home to several unusual museums that offer unique and intriguing experiences beyond the traditional museum visit. The Cat Cabinet (Kattenkabinet), dedicated to art featuring cats, is housed in a beautiful canal house and is a delight for cat enthusiasts. Another quirky museum is the Electric Ladyland, the first museum of fluorescent art, offering an immersive and colorful experience.

For those interested in the city's history, the Museum Vrolik, located within the Amsterdam University Medical Center, displays an extensive collection of anatomical specimens and medical oddities. These unusual museums not only provide a fascinating glimpse into niche topics but also highlight Amsterdam's diverse cultural offerings.

When planning to visit these museums, check their opening hours as some have limited visiting times. These unique museums are ideal for those looking to explore the quirkier side of Amsterdam's culture and history.

Day Trip to Utrecht

A day trip to Utrecht, a charming city located just a short train ride from Amsterdam, offers a delightful experience with its medieval architecture, scenic canals, and vibrant cultural scene. Utrecht's old town is dominated by the Dom Tower, the tallest church tower in the Netherlands, which provides panoramic views of the city.

Utrecht is known for its picturesque canals with wharf cellars housing cafes and restaurants along the water, creating a unique dining experience. The city is also rich in arts and culture, with several museums and galleries, including the Centraal Museum and the Museum Speelklok, showcasing a collection of automatically playing musical instruments.

Exploring Utrecht's historic streets, relaxing by the canals, and visiting its cultural attractions make for a perfect day away from the bustle of Amsterdam. Utrecht's smaller scale and less touristy atmosphere provide a more laid-back experience, allowing visitors to immerse themselves in Dutch city life.

Final Thoughts

Exploring the less trodden paths of Amsterdam reveals a city rich in hidden treasures and quiet charms. This chapter has taken you through serene courtyards, unusual museums, and tranquil green spaces, showing a side of Amsterdam that often goes unnoticed by the typical tourist crowd. These off-the-beaten-path experiences provide a deeper understanding of Amsterdam's diverse character and history, offering a more intimate connection with the city.

As you venture beyond the main attractions, consider the countless small wonders that Amsterdam has to offer. Take time to wander through lesser-known neighborhoods, where local life unfolds in its most authentic form. Enjoy the calm of the city's hidden gardens, the quirky appeal of its unusual museums, and the quaint beauty of its quieter streets and canals.

Remember, exploring these lesser-known parts of Amsterdam not only enriches your travel experience but also helps distribute tourist traffic more evenly, contributing to the preservation of the city's charm and livability. Be mindful of your impact as a visitor and embrace the opportunity to discover Amsterdam's quieter side.

Finally, don't hesitate to strike up conversations with locals. They can often provide valuable insights and recommendations for hidden gems and local favorites that are not found in guidebooks. By stepping off the beaten path, you open yourself up to experiences that are both unique and memorable, capturing the true essence of Amsterdam's captivating spirit.

CHAPTER 10:
Amsterdam Through the Seasons

Amsterdam, a city renowned for its picturesque canals and historic architecture, offers a different charm in each season. In this chapter, we explore the unique beauty and activities that each season brings to Amsterdam. From the vibrant tulip blooms of spring to the festive atmosphere of winter, the city adapts and transforms, offering varied experiences to its visitors and residents alike. Understanding what each season has to offer can help you plan your visit to make the most of Amsterdam's ever-changing landscape.

As you journey through the seasons in Amsterdam, remember that each brings its own weather patterns and cultural events. This chapter will guide you through what to expect and how to prepare for each season, ensuring a delightful and fulfilling experience in this dynamic city.

Spring in Amsterdam

Spring in Amsterdam is a time of renewal and celebration, as the city shakes off the winter chill and welcomes the warmth of the new season. The most iconic symbol of spring in Amsterdam is undoubtedly the tulip. The city and surrounding countryside burst into color with blooming tulips and other spring flowers. A visit to the Keukenhof Gardens, although a bit outside the city, is a must for flower enthusiasts.

Spring is also the season of King's Day (Koningsdag), celebrated on April 27th. The city comes alive with street parties, canal parades, and markets. The atmosphere is joyous and vibrant, with residents and visitors alike dressed in orange, the national color.

When planning a spring visit, pack layers as the weather can be unpredictable. Enjoy strolling through the city parks, such as Vondelpark or Amstelpark, which are at their most beautiful during this season. The longer daylight hours and milder weather make spring an ideal time for outdoor activities and exploring the city's many outdoor markets and festivals.

Summer in Amsterdam

Summer in Amsterdam is a lively and bustling time, with long days and an abundance of outdoor activities. The city's numerous terraces, rooftop bars, and outdoor cafes are filled with locals and tourists enjoying the sunny weather. Summer is perfect for exploring Amsterdam's canals by boat, whether on a guided tour or renting a private boat for a more personal experience.

Cultural festivals and outdoor events are plentiful in summer. The Grachtenfestival, a classical music festival held on and around the canals, is a highlight, as well as the open-air cinema screenings and numerous food and music festivals.

For a summer visit, be prepared for warm weather, and consider bringing a hat and sunscreen. It's also advisable to book accommodations and attractions in advance, as this is a popular time for tourists. Take advantage of the long days by exploring the city's vibrant neighborhoods and relaxing in its beautiful parks, such as the Westerpark or the Amsterdamse Bos, which offer a range of summer activities.

Autumn in Amsterdam

Autumn in Amsterdam is a season of stunning beauty and cultural vibrancy. The city's parks and canals transform with hues of orange and gold, offering picturesque scenes at every turn. It's a perfect time for leisurely walks or bike rides to admire the changing foliage, especially in areas like the Amsterdamse Bos or along the Amstel River.

This season is also marked by cultural events, including the Amsterdam Dance Event (ADE) and the Museum Night (Museumnacht), where museums across the city open their doors late into the night with special programs and exhibitions. The cooler weather of autumn is ideal for exploring indoor attractions like museums and galleries.

When visiting Amsterdam in autumn, packing layers is advisable as the weather can be quite variable. It's also a great time to enjoy the city's cozy cafes and restaurants, where you can warm up with a hot drink or a hearty meal. The autumn months are generally less crowded, offering a more relaxed atmosphere for experiencing the city's cultural offerings.

Winter in Amsterdam

Winter in Amsterdam is a magical time, with the city illuminated by festive lights and decorations. The colder months bring unique experiences like the Amsterdam Light Festival, where contemporary light artworks are displayed throughout the city. Ice-skating rinks pop up in various locations, including the well-known rink at Museumplein, set against the stunning backdrop of the Rijksmuseum.

The holiday season in Amsterdam is festive and lively. Traditional Dutch winter treats like oliebollen (deep-fried dough balls) and speculaas (spiced cookies) are a must-try. Christmas markets, such as those at Rembrandtplein and Leidseplein, offer a cheerful atmosphere with stalls selling gifts, food, and mulled wine.

For winter travel, warm clothing and waterproof gear are essential, as the weather can be cold and damp. Winter is also a great time to enjoy Amsterdam's indoor attractions, including its renowned theaters and concert halls, which host a variety of performances during this season.

Dining Out

Amsterdam's culinary scene shines in every season, offering a range of dining experiences from cozy winter meals to al fresco summer dining. The city's diverse restaurant scene caters to all tastes, with options ranging from traditional Dutch cuisine to international dishes.

In spring and summer, the outdoor terraces of cafes and restaurants are particularly popular, allowing diners to enjoy their meals in the vibrant street atmosphere. Autumn and winter bring the opportunity to experience the gezelligheid (coziness) of Amsterdam's dining establishments, with many restaurants offering seasonal specialties and warm, inviting interiors.

When dining out in Amsterdam, consider trying seasonal local dishes, such as stamppot in winter or asparagus in spring. The city's markets are also great places to sample local street food and fresh produce. Regardless of the season, Amsterdam offers a delightful culinary journey, reflecting the city's multicultural spirit and rich gastronomic heritage.

Seasonal Shopping

Shopping in Amsterdam varies delightfully with the seasons, offering different experiences throughout the year. In spring and summer, markets and boutiques overflow with vibrant colors, selling everything from fresh flowers, like the famous Dutch tulips, to lightweight fashion ideal for the warmer months. Outdoor markets such as the Albert Cuypmarkt or the Bloemenmarkt, the world's only floating flower market, are particularly enjoyable during these seasons.

Autumn brings a shift to warmer clothing and accessories, with many shops displaying the latest trends in fall fashion. It's a great time to explore Amsterdam's vintage and second-hand shops for unique finds. As winter sets in, the shopping focus turns to holiday gifts and decorations. The city's Christmas markets are perfect for finding unique gifts, handmade crafts, and seasonal treats. When shopping in Amsterdam, consider the weather and local festivities to make the most of seasonal offerings. Also, be on the lookout for seasonal sales, particularly during the end of winter and summer, when many stores offer significant discounts.

Cultural Activities

Each season in Amsterdam brings a variety of cultural activities that cater to diverse interests. Spring often features art exhibitions and cultural festivals, taking advantage of the milder weather.

Summer is ideal for open-air concerts and cinema screenings, such as those held at Vondelpark or along the city's canals.

Autumn's cooler temperatures are perfect for exploring Amsterdam's renowned museums and galleries, many of which launch new exhibitions during this time. Winter in Amsterdam is rich with cultural experiences, from the Amsterdam Light Festival to holiday concerts and performances.

Regardless of the season, it's advisable to check the city's cultural calendar for events and exhibitions. Participating in these cultural activities not only enriches your visit but also provides deeper insight into Amsterdam's artistic and cultural landscape.

Festivals and Traditions

Amsterdam's festivals and traditions vary with the seasons, reflecting the city's vibrant cultural life. Spring celebrations such as King's Day (Koningsdag) in April and the National Tulip Day in January bring the city to life with color and excitement. Summer is marked by events like Pride Amsterdam, with its famous Canal Parade, and various music festivals.

Autumn sees the celebration of cultural events like the Amsterdam Dance Event and Museum Night, while winter is highlighted by traditional Dutch festivities like Sinterklaas in December and the New Year's Eve celebrations. The winter months also feature unique Dutch traditions, including the arrival of Sinterklaas and his helpers in November.

Engaging in these seasonal festivals and traditions offers a glimpse into the Dutch way of life and allows visitors to fully immerse themselves in the local culture. Each festival has its own charm and significance, providing visitors with a rich and varied experience of Amsterdam's cultural heritage.

Practical Tips

When visiting Amsterdam through the seasons, a few practical tips can enhance your experience. Firstly, always check the weather forecast and pack accordingly. Amsterdam's weather can be unpredictable, and having the right clothing will ensure you're comfortable exploring the city.

In spring, bring layers and a raincoat to handle the mild yet sometimes rainy weather. Summer calls for light clothing, sunglasses, and sunscreen, as the days can be warm and sunny. For autumn, pack warm layers and a sturdy umbrella, as this season can be cool and wet. Winter requires warm clothing, including a heavy coat, gloves, and a hat, to stay cozy during the colder months.

Secondly, consider purchasing an I amsterdam City Card, which offers free or discounted entry to many attractions and museums, as well as unlimited use of public transportation. This can be especially useful for exploring the city's cultural offerings throughout the year.

Finally, be mindful of national holidays and school vacations, as these can affect opening hours of attractions and lead to busier periods in the city.

Final Thoughts

Exploring Amsterdam through the seasons offers a dynamic and ever-changing experience of the city. Each season brings its own unique beauty and opportunities, from the vibrant tulips of spring to the festive lights of winter. By understanding what each season has to offer, you can tailor your visit to align with your interests, whether it's attending summer festivals, enjoying the autumnal art scene, exploring springtime parks, or experiencing winter traditions.

Remember, each season in Amsterdam has its own charm and is worth experiencing. The city's adaptability to the changing seasons is a testament to its vibrant and resilient spirit. No matter when you choose to visit, Amsterdam promises a rich tapestry of experiences, leaving you with lasting memories of this beautiful and diverse city.

AMSTERDAM TRAVEL GUIDE

CHAPTER 11:
How to Travel Amsterdam on a Budget
· · · · · · · · · · · · · · · · · · · ·

Traveling to Amsterdam on a budget is entirely feasible with some planning and savvy choices. This chapter will guide you through various ways to enjoy the city without breaking the bank. From finding affordable accommodation to eating well on a budget, Amsterdam offers plenty of options for budget-conscious travelers. Embracing the city's affordable offerings doesn't mean compromising on the experience; it simply means traveling smarter and getting creative with how you explore Amsterdam.

Budget travel in Amsterdam is about making informed choices and looking for value. This chapter will provide tips and insights to help you navigate the city economically while still soaking up its rich culture and vibrant atmosphere.

Budget Accommodation

Finding budget accommodation in Amsterdam requires some research and flexibility. Hostels are a great option, offering not only affordable rates but also opportunities to meet fellow travelers. Many hostels in Amsterdam provide amenities like free Wi-Fi, communal kitchens, and even complimentary breakfasts. The Flying Pig and Stayokay are popular hostel chains in the city known for their cleanliness and friendly atmosphere.

Another budget-friendly option is to consider short-term rental apartments or staying in local neighborhoods outside the city center, where accommodation tends to be less expensive. Websites like Airbnb and Booking.com can be useful for finding these deals.

When looking for budget accommodation, it's advisable to book well in advance, especially during peak tourist seasons. Also, consider staying near public transport routes to save on travel costs while still having easy access to the city's main attractions.

Eating on a Budget

Eating on a budget in Amsterdam doesn't mean you have to miss out on delicious food. The city offers a range of affordable dining options, from street food and markets to cozy cafes. Street food like herring sandwiches, stroopwafels, and Dutch fries are not only inexpensive but also offer a taste of local flavors.

Markets like Albert Cuypmarkt and De Pijp offer fresh produce and a variety of food stalls where you can enjoy affordable and authentic meals. Many restaurants also offer 'dagmenu' (daily menu) or 'hapjes' (small bites), which are cost-effective ways to try different dishes.

To save on dining costs, consider having your main meal during lunch when many restaurants offer lunch specials at lower prices than dinner. Also, self-catering by shopping at local supermarkets and using hostel kitchens can significantly reduce your food expenses. Remember, part of the fun of traveling is exploring local foods, and Amsterdam offers plenty of tasty options that won't strain your budget.

Public Transport

Navigating Amsterdam efficiently and economically is possible with the city's excellent public transport system. The GVB, Amsterdam's public transport company, operates trams, buses, and metros that cover the entire city and beyond. Purchasing a multi-day transport pass, such as the Amsterdam Travel Ticket or the I amsterdam City Card, can offer unlimited travel and be more cost-effective than single tickets.

Biking is another budget-friendly and quintessentially Dutch way to get around Amsterdam. The city's flat terrain and extensive network of bike lanes make cycling safe and enjoyable. Bike rentals are available throughout the city at reasonable rates, and many hostels even offer bikes for rent to their guests.

For budget travelers, it's advisable to plan your routes using public transport or bike to avoid the higher costs of taxis. Apps like Google Maps and 9292.nl provide real-time public transport information and can help you navigate the city easily.

Free Attractions

Amsterdam offers numerous free attractions, allowing budget travelers to enjoy the city's culture and beauty without spending a dime. Walking along the iconic canals, exploring the historic Jordaan neighborhood, or visiting the bustling Dam Square are all free and offer an authentic Amsterdam experience.

The city also boasts beautiful parks such as Vondelpark and Westerpark, perfect for a leisurely stroll or a picnic. Additionally, many of Amsterdam's churches, including the St. Nicholas Church near Amsterdam Centraal, are free to enter and explore. Keep an eye out for free events and festivals, particularly in the summer months. Many museums and galleries also offer free entry on certain days or times, so check their schedules in advance. Exploring these free attractions is a wonderful way to immerse yourself in Amsterdam's vibrant culture without spending money.

Budget Shopping

Shopping in Amsterdam doesn't have to be an expensive endeavor. The city offers several markets where you can find bargains, from vintage clothes to unique souvenirs. The Waterlooplein Flea Market and the IJ-Hallen, Europe's largest flea market, are great places to hunt for second-hand goods and antiques at reasonable prices.

For budget-friendly fashion, explore the Nine Streets (De Negen Straatjes) and the area around Haarlemmerstraat, where you can find a mix of vintage shops and affordable boutiques. Additionally, many stores in Amsterdam offer seasonal sales, particularly in January and July, when you can find significant discounts.

When shopping on a budget, always compare prices and don't hesitate to explore the city's less touristy neighborhoods, where prices tend to be lower. Markets and local shops not only offer affordable shopping options but also provide a glimpse into the daily life of Amsterdammers.

Cheap Flight and Train Tips

Securing cheap flights and train travel to Amsterdam can significantly reduce your overall travel costs. For flights, consider booking well in advance or being flexible with your travel dates. Utilizing fare comparison websites and setting fare alerts can also help you find the best deals. Low-cost airlines often offer competitive prices, but be sure to check for additional fees for baggage or seat selection.

When traveling within Europe, consider taking a train to Amsterdam. The city is well-connected by rail, and early bookings can yield substantial savings. Look for special offers and discounts on train tickets, especially if you have a flexible schedule. Overnight trains can also be a cost-effective option, saving you a night's accommodation.

Discount Cards

Utilizing discount cards can lead to significant savings on attractions and dining in Amsterdam. The I Amsterdam City Card is a popular choice, offering free entry to many museums and attractions, unlimited use of GVB public transport, and discounts at restaurants and shops. Another option is the Holland Pass, which provides discounted or free entry to top attractions in Amsterdam and other cities in the Netherlands.

When considering a discount card, evaluate your itinerary to ensure that the card aligns with the places you plan to visit. These cards can be particularly valuable for travelers interested in experiencing multiple museums and cultural sites.

Off-Season Travel

Traveling to Amsterdam during the off-season – typically from late autumn to early spring – can be more budget-friendly. During these months, accommodation rates are often lower, and the city is less crowded, allowing for a more relaxed experience. The off-season also brings unique charms, such as the Amsterdam Light Festival in winter and the city's beautiful autumn foliage.

While some outdoor activities may be limited in the off-season, many of Amsterdam's attractions, including museums and historical sites, can be fully enjoyed year-round. Additionally, visiting during the off-season provides an opportunity to experience local festivals and events that are not as well known to tourists.

Budget-Friendly Activities

Engaging in budget-friendly activities is a great way to enjoy Amsterdam without overspending. One of the best ways to explore the city is by taking a self-guided walking tour. Maps and apps are available to guide you through Amsterdam's historical streets, landmarks, and neighborhoods at no cost. Additionally, the city is home to many free galleries and street art installations, particularly in neighborhoods like Jordaan and NDSM Wharf, offering a glimpse into Amsterdam's vibrant art scene.

Many of Amsterdam's parks, including Vondelpark, Westerpark, and Amsterdamse Bos, are free to visit and host various events and activities throughout the year. Picnicking, bird-watching, or simply enjoying a leisurely walk in these parks are excellent ways to spend a day.

Another budget-friendly activity is attending open mic nights, free concerts, or jam sessions at local bars and clubs. These events are often free or have a very low entrance fee, providing affordable entertainment options.

Final Thoughts

Exploring Amsterdam on a budget is not only possible but can also lead to a more authentic experience of the city. By staying in budget accommodations, eating at affordable eateries, using cost-effective transport options, and engaging in free or low-cost activities, you can enjoy the essence of Amsterdam without a hefty price tag.

Remember, the key to budget travel in Amsterdam is planning and flexibility. Researching in advance, taking advantage of discount cards, and traveling during the off-season can significantly reduce costs. Moreover, exploring off-the-beaten-path attractions and immersing yourself in the local culture can be enriching experiences that are often more affordable.

Amsterdam's beauty and charm are not confined to its expensive attractions. The city offers a wealth of experiences that are accessible to travelers of all budgets. With a little creativity and resourcefulness, you can discover the many facets of this captivating city without compromising the quality of your visit.

CHAPTER 12:
10 Cultural Experiences You Must Try in Amsterdam

Amsterdam's cultural landscape is as rich and varied as its history, offering a myriad of experiences that reflect the artistic and creative spirit of the city. This chapter explores ten cultural experiences that are quintessentially Dutch and provide an immersive insight into Amsterdam's artistic heritage. From the world of cinema and music to the enchanting realm of theatre, these experiences are essential for anyone looking to engage deeply with the city's cultural heartbeat.

Each of these cultural experiences offers a unique perspective on Amsterdam's artistic contributions and will enrich your understanding of the city's vibrant cultural scene. Whether you are an art enthusiast, a music lover, or a theatre aficionado, Amsterdam has something captivating to offer.

1 - Dutch Cinema

Dutch cinema, known for its unique storytelling and innovative filmmaking, offers a distinctive cinematic experience. In Amsterdam, venues like The Eye Film Museum and The Movies provide opportunities to explore Dutch and international films. The Eye Film Museum, in particular, is a hub for film lovers, with its extensive archive, exhibitions, and screenings of both classic and contemporary films.

Many of Amsterdam's cinemas host film festivals throughout the year, showcasing Dutch films and offering Q&A sessions with filmmakers. These festivals are a great way to dive into the world of Dutch cinema and experience the diversity of its storytelling.

To immerse yourself in Dutch cinema, consider attending screenings of Dutch films with English subtitles. This experience will not only provide entertainment but also offer insights into Dutch culture and social issues. Keep an eye out for film festivals like IDFA (International Documentary Film Festival Amsterdam) for a comprehensive cinematic experience.

2 - Dutch Music

The Dutch music scene in Amsterdam spans a wide range of genres, from classical and jazz to electronic and pop. Renowned venues like Paradiso and Melkweg host performances by both local and international artists, offering a lively and diverse music experience.

Amsterdam also boasts a strong tradition in classical music, with the Royal Concertgebouw being one of the world's leading concert halls. Attending a concert here, whether it's the resident orchestra or a visiting ensemble, is a must for classical music enthusiasts.

For a more casual music experience, explore the city's jazz clubs and live music bars, where you can enjoy performances in an intimate setting. Checking out local music festivals, such as Amsterdam Music Festival and JazzFest Amsterdam, can also be a delightful way to experience the vibrancy of the Dutch music scene.

3 - Dutch Theatre

Amsterdam's theatre scene is vibrant and dynamic, offering a range of performances from traditional Dutch plays to modern experimental productions. Major theatres like Stadsschouwburg and DeLaMar Theater host a variety of plays, dance performances, and operas, often with English surtitles or translations available.

For a taste of contemporary Dutch theatre, visit smaller venues like Frascati or De Brakke Grond, which showcase innovative and cutting-edge performances. These theatres often focus on new works by Dutch playwrights and directors, providing a fresh perspective on modern theatre.

To fully engage with Dutch theatre, consider attending a performance at the annual Holland Festival, which features a selection of theatre, music, dance, and opera from around the world. This festival is an excellent opportunity to experience the diversity and creativity of Amsterdam's theatre scene.

4 - Dutch Literature

Dutch literature, with its rich history and contemporary vibrancy, offers a window into the soul of the Netherlands. Amsterdam, in particular, is a city of writers and readers, with numerous bookshops and literary events. Visiting the renowned bookstores like Athenaeum Boekhandel and The American Book Center can be a delight for book lovers, offering a range of works by Dutch authors, many available in English translations. Amsterdam also hosts literary festivals and author readings, providing opportunities to delve deeper into Dutch literature. The city's public libraries, especially the central OBA (Openbare Bibliotheek Amsterdam), regularly organize literary events and discussions.

For a more immersive experience, consider joining a literary walking tour that takes you through locations associated with famous Dutch writers and poets. These tours offer insights into the lives of authors and the settings of their works, bringing Dutch literature to life in the streets of Amsterdam.

5 - Cheese Tasting

Cheese tasting is an essential experience in Amsterdam, given the Netherlands' rich cheese-making tradition. The city offers numerous cheese shops and markets where you can sample a variety of Dutch cheeses, such as Gouda, Edam, and Leyden. Specialty cheese shops like Reypenaer and De Kaaskamer provide guided cheese tastings, allowing you to savor different flavors and learn about the cheese-making process.

Many cheese shops also offer pairings with Dutch wines or beers, enhancing the tasting experience. A visit to the local markets, such as Albert Cuypmarkt, will also give you a chance to taste and buy cheese directly from the producers.

For a comprehensive cheese experience, consider taking a day trip to the nearby cheese markets in towns like Alkmaar or Edam, especially during the summer months when traditional cheese markets are held.

6 - Cycling Tours

Cycling is an integral part of Amsterdam's culture, and joining a cycling tour is a fantastic way to explore the city like a local. Numerous companies offer guided bike tours, taking you through the city's main attractions as well as less-known neighborhoods. These tours can provide insights into Amsterdam's history, architecture, and lifestyle, all while enjoying the city's bike-friendly infrastructure.

For those who prefer independent exploration, renting a bike and following one of the many cycling routes around the city is a great option. Maps and apps are available to guide you along scenic routes, such as those through the Amsterdamse Bos or along the Amstel River.

When cycling in Amsterdam, remember to follow local cycling rules and be mindful of both pedestrians and vehicular traffic. Cycling tours are not only a way to see the city but also a chance to experience Amsterdam's commitment to sustainable and active transportation.

7 - Dutch Language

Learning a few phrases in Dutch can greatly enrich your Amsterdam experience, allowing for a deeper connection with locals and the city's culture. While many Amsterdammers speak excellent English, showing interest in the local language is always appreciated. Consider taking a short Dutch language course offered by language schools in the city, or join a language exchange meetup where you can practice speaking with locals.

Many cafes and bookshops sell beginner-friendly Dutch language guides and phrasebooks that can be handy during your stay. Additionally, smartphone apps can also be a quick and effective way to learn basic Dutch phrases and greetings.

Engaging with the Dutch language, even on a basic level, can open up new aspects of Amsterdam's culture and lifestyle.

Simple conversations with locals in Dutch, even if just greetings or thank-yous, can add a layer of authenticity to your visit and often lead to more meaningful interactions.

8 - Dutch Coffee Shop

Visiting a Dutch coffee shop in Amsterdam offers a unique cultural experience, as these establishments are known for selling cannabis products in a regulated environment. It's an integral part of Amsterdam's contemporary culture, reflecting the city's liberal and tolerant attitude. When visiting a coffee shop, it's important to understand and respect the local laws and customs related to cannabis use.

Many coffee shops in Amsterdam offer a relaxed atmosphere where you can learn about different cannabis strains and their effects from knowledgeable staff. However, always consume responsibly and be aware of the effects, especially if you are inexperienced.

Exploring the coffee shop scene can be an interesting cultural experience, but remember, it's just one aspect of what Amsterdam has to offer. Always be respectful of the local community and other patrons while visiting these establishments.

9 - Dutch Festivals

Amsterdam's festival calendar is packed with events celebrating everything from music and art to food and heritage. Engaging in these festivals is a fantastic way to experience Dutch culture. King's Day (Koningsdag) in April transforms the city into a vibrant orange sea with street parties and flea markets.

The Grachtenfestival in August features classical music performances along the canals.

For film enthusiasts, the International Documentary Film Festival Amsterdam (IDFA) in November is a major event, while art lovers should not miss the Amsterdam Art Weekend. The summer months are filled with music festivals catering to all tastes, from electronic to jazz.

Participating in these festivals allows you to experience the Dutch spirit of celebration and enjoy the diversity of cultural expressions. Check the festival schedules in advance and partake in these lively events that showcase the richness of Amsterdam's cultural scene.

10 - Dutch Architecture

Exploring Dutch architecture in Amsterdam is a journey through centuries of design and innovation. The city is renowned for its historical buildings as well as modern architectural marvels. A walk through Amsterdam reveals a diverse array of architectural styles, from the narrow gabled houses of the Golden Age along the canals to the cutting-edge designs in areas like the Eastern Docklands and IJburg.

One of the key architectural highlights is the Amsterdam School style, best exemplified in buildings like Het Schip and the Scheepvaarthuis. These structures are noted for their decorative brickwork, intricate masonry, and organic forms. For contemporary architecture enthusiasts, the EYE Film Museum and NEMO Science Museum are modern landmarks with striking designs.

To deepen your appreciation of Dutch architecture, consider joining a guided architectural tour or visiting one of the city's architecture centers, such as ARCAM, which offers exhibitions and information on Amsterdam's urban development.

Amsterdam's architecture is not just about aesthetics; it reflects the city's history, culture, and ongoing commitment to innovative urban design. Exploring these architectural wonders provides a unique perspective on Amsterdam and its evolution from a 13th-century fishing village to a modern, vibrant metropolis.

CHAPTER 13:
Amsterdam Walks and Bike Rides

Amsterdam, a city celebrated for its scenic canals and charming streets, is best explored on foot or by bike. This chapter invites you on a journey through Amsterdam's picturesque lanes and waterways, guiding you through walks and bike rides that capture the essence of the city. Whether strolling through historic neighborhoods or cycling along serene canals, these self-guided tours provide an intimate glimpse into Amsterdam's beauty and lifestyle.

Walking and biking in Amsterdam are not just modes of transportation; they are experiences that allow you to connect with the city's rhythm and discover hidden gems at your own pace. This chapter will help you uncover the lesser-known corners of Amsterdam and appreciate the city's unique charm and character.

Tips for Walking and Cycling in Amsterdam

Amsterdam's compact size and flat terrain make it ideal for walking and cycling. Here are some tips to help you enjoy these activities safely and comfortably:

Walking Tips:

Wear comfortable shoes as Amsterdam's cobbled streets and canalside paths can be uneven.

Always be aware of your surroundings, especially of cyclists and trams.

Utilize maps or GPS on your mobile device to navigate, but also don't be afraid to wander and discover unexpected delights.

Cycling Tips:

Rent a bike from one of the many bike rental shops around the city. Make sure you're comfortable with the bike's size and controls.

Follow the cycling rules: use bike lanes, signal your turns, and always lock your bike.

Be mindful of pedestrians and other traffic, especially in busy areas like the city center.

Both walking and cycling offer environmentally friendly ways to explore Amsterdam and allow for a more immersive experience. Whether you're meandering through the Jordaan or pedaling through the Vondelpark, each step or pedal stroke brings you closer to the heart of Amsterdam.

1 - Historic City Center Walk

- Duration: 2 hours
- Difficulty: Easy
- Start: Amsterdam Centraal Station
- End: Dam Square

. . . .

Route

Begin at Amsterdam Centraal Station, heading towards the Damrak.
Explore the bustling Damrak and visit Beurs van Berlage.
Walk to Dam Square, home to the Royal Palace and National Monument.
Stroll through the alleys of the Red Light District.
Finish at Dam Square, exploring nearby shopping streets.

Points of Interest

- Beurs van Berlage
- Dam Square
- Royal Palace
- Red Light District

. . . .

2 - Jordaan Neighborhood Walk

- ▸ Duration: 2-3 hours
- ▸ Difficulty: Easy
- ▸ Start: Westerkerk
- ▸ End: Noordermarkt

. . . .

Route

Start at Westerkerk, near Anne Frank House.
Walk along the Prinsengracht canal, admiring the historic houses.
Explore the quaint streets of Jordaan, filled with boutiques and cafes.
Visit the Houseboat Museum along the way.
End at the Noordermarkt, a great place for a coffee or snack.

Points of Interest

- ▸ Westerkerk
- ▸ Prinsengracht canal
- ▸ Houseboat Museum
- ▸ Noordermarkt

. . . .

3 - Canal Ring Walk

- ▶ Duration: 2 hours
- ▶ Difficulty: Easy
- ▶ Start: Leidseplein
- ▶ End: Rembrandtplein

Route

Begin at Leidseplein, walking towards the Keizersgracht canal.
Follow Keizersgracht to the famous Seven Bridges viewpoint.
Continue to the Herengracht canal, admiring the elegant canal houses.
Walk towards Rembrandtplein, exploring the side streets and boutiques.
Finish at Rembrandtplein, a lively square with many cafes.

Points of Interest

- ▶ Leidseplein
- ▶ Seven Bridges viewpoint
- ▶ Herengracht canal
- ▶ Rembrandtplein

4 - De Pijp Neighborhood Walk

- ▸ Duration: 1-2 hours
- ▸ Difficulty: Easy
- ▸ Start: Albert Cuyp Market
- ▸ End: Sarphatipark

. . . .

Route

Start at the vibrant Albert Cuyp Market.
Explore the streets of De Pijp, known for their diverse food and shops.
Visit the Heineken Experience if interested in beer history.
Stroll through the Sarphatipark for some green space.
End the walk at the Sarphatipark, perfect for a relaxing break.

Points of Interest

- ▸ Albert Cuyp Market
- ▸ Heineken Experience
- ▸ Sarphatipark
- ▸ Bike Rides in Amsterdam

. . . .

5 - Vondelpark and Museum Quarter Ride

- ▶ Duration: 1-2 hours
- ▶ Difficulty: Easy
- ▶ Start and End: Vondelpark

• •

Route

Cycle around Vondelpark, the largest city park in Amsterdam.
Head towards the Museum Quarter, passing by the Rijksmuseum and Van Gogh Museum.
Explore the chic streets of the Oud-Zuid neighborhood.
Loop back to Vondelpark for more leisurely cycling or a good picnic.

Points of Interest

- ▶ Vondelpark
- ▶ Rijksmuseum
- ▶ Van Gogh Museum
- ▶ Oud-Zuid neighborhood

• •

6 - Amsterdamse Bos Ride

▶ Duration: 2-3 hours
▶ Difficulty: Easy/Moderate
▶ Start and End: Amsterdamse Bos

. . . .

Route

Start at the entrance of Amsterdamse Bos, a large forested park.
Cycle through the park, exploring its lakes, open meadows, and
wooded areas.
Visit the goat farm and the open-air theater if open.
Enjoy the numerous bike paths within the park, offering scenic
views.

Points of Interest

▶ Amsterdamse Bos
▶ Goat Farm
▶ Open-air Theater

. . . .

7 - River Amstel Ride

- ▶ Duration: 2-3 hours
- ▶ Difficulty: Moderate
- ▶ Start: De Magere Brug
- ▶ End: Ouderkerk aan de Amstel

. . . .

Route

Begin at the Magere Brug (Skinny Bridge) and head south along the Amstel River.

Pass by iconic windmills and the Dutch countryside.

Stop at the quaint village of Ouderkerk aan de Amstel for a break.

Cycle back to Amsterdam or explore further along the river.

Points of Interest

- ▶ De Magere Brug
- ▶ Windmills along the Amstel
- ▶ Ouderkerk aan de Amstel

. . . .

8 - North Amsterdam Ride

- ▶ Duration: 2-3 hours
- ▶ Difficulty: Easy/Moderate
- ▶ Start and End: Amsterdam Central Station (take ferry to North)

....

Route

Take the ferry from Central Station to Amsterdam Noord.
Cycle through the trendy NDSM Wharf area, known for its street art.
Explore the rural landscapes and villages in the northern part of the city.
Return to the ferry and head back to Central Station.

Points of Interest

- ▶ NDSM Wharf
- ▶ Amsterdam Noord rural areas
- ▶ Ferry ride across the IJ river

....

AMSTERDAM TRAVEL GUIDE

CHAPTER 14:
Recommended Itinerary in Amsterdam

Amsterdam, with its enchanting canals, rich history, and vibrant culture, offers an array of experiences to suit every traveler. This chapter is designed to help you make the most of your time in the city, whether you're visiting for a weekend or a week. Here, we provide a recommended itinerary that covers the must-see attractions as well as some hidden gems, ensuring a well-rounded experience of Amsterdam.

Our itinerary is structured to allow for a balance of sightseeing, relaxation, and exploration. It's flexible, allowing you to adapt it based on your interests and the length of your stay. By following this guide, you'll be able to explore the best of Amsterdam and discover why this city captivates the hearts of all who wander its storied streets.

Planning Your Trip

When planning your trip to Amsterdam, consider a few key factors to ensure a smooth and enjoyable experience. Firstly, decide on the duration of your stay. Amsterdam can be explored over a weekend, but a longer stay allows you to delve deeper into the city's culture and neighborhoods.

Accommodation is plentiful in Amsterdam, ranging from luxury hotels to cozy hostels. Booking in advance, especially during peak tourist seasons, is advisable to secure the best rates and locations. Staying near the city center or close to a major transit hub can save time and make sightseeing more convenient. Lastly, consider purchasing a travel pass like the I amsterdam City Card, which offers free or discounted entry to many attractions and unlimited use of public transport. Also, familiarize yourself with the city's public transportation system to navigate easily between different sights and neighborhoods. Balancing planned activities with free time for spontaneous exploration will help make your Amsterdam adventure both fulfilling and memorable.

3-Day Itinerary in Amsterdam

Day 1:

▶ **Morning**: Start your Amsterdam adventure by visiting the iconic Anne Frank House. It's advisable to book tickets in advance. After this moving experience, take a leisurely stroll around the Jordaan neighborhood, known for its picturesque streets and hidden courtyards.

▶ **Afternoon**: Head to the bustling Dam Square and visit the Royal Palace. Then, enjoy a relaxing canal cruise to see the city from its famous waterways. Cruises often start near the Anne Frank House or Central Station.

▶ **Evening**: Explore the vibrant De Pijp neighborhood. Have dinner at one of the many ethnic restaurants in the area, then end your day with a visit to a cozy brown café.

Day 2:

▶ **Morning**: Visit the Rijksmuseum to see masterpieces of Dutch art, including works by Rembrandt and Vermeer. Spend a few hours exploring the museum's extensive collection.

▶ **Afternoon**: Take a walk in the nearby Vondelpark, Amsterdam's largest city park. Afterward, explore the upscale shopping streets in the Oud-Zuid neighborhood or visit the nearby Van Gogh Museum.

- **Evening**: Head to the lively Leidseplein area for dinner, followed by a night out at one of the area's many bars or theaters.

Day 3:

- **Morning**: Start your day in the historic city center. Visit the bustling Albert Cuyp Market in De Pijp, then head to the nearby Heineken Experience for a tour of the famous brewery.

- **Afternoon**: Spend your afternoon in the medieval core of Amsterdam. Visit the Oude Kerk (Old Church), stroll through the Red Light District, and explore the charming streets around the Nieuwmarkt.

- **Evening**: For your final evening, dine in the atmospheric Jordaan district and enjoy live music at one of the local bars.

5-Day Itinerary in Amsterdam

Day 4:

- **Morning**: Take a day trip to the picturesque village of Zaanse Schans. Explore traditional Dutch windmills, wooden houses, and a clog-making demonstration.

- **Afternoon**: Return to Amsterdam and spend the afternoon shopping in the Nine Streets (De Negen Straatjes), known for their boutique shops and vintage stores.

- **Evening**: Enjoy a fine dining experience at one of Amsterdam's gourmet restaurants in the city center.

Day 5:

- **Morning**: Visit the Hortus Botanicus, one of the oldest botanical gardens in the world. Then, explore the nearby Jewish Quarter, including the Jewish Historical Museum and the Portuguese Synagogue.

- **Afternoon**: Spend your last afternoon in Amsterdam at the modern art museum, Stedelijk, or relax with a coffee in the Museumplein area.

- **Evening**: Conclude your visit with a stroll along the historic canals in the Grachtengordel area, followed by a farewell drink on a canal-side terrace.

Conclusion

As we reach the conclusion of our Amsterdam travel guide, we take a moment to reflect on the unique essence of this remarkable city. Amsterdam, with its intricate network of canals, historic architecture, and vibrant cultural scene, offers a multifaceted experience that goes far beyond the usual tourist attractions. It's a city where history intertwines with modern lifestyle, where art and innovation coexist seamlessly, and where the spirit of freedom and tolerance is palpable in every street and canal.

Amsterdam is more than just a destination; it's a living tapestry of experiences waiting to be discovered. Whether it's the peaceful bike rides along leafy pathways, the cozy ambiance of a brown café, or the thrill of exploring cutting-edge art in a converted warehouse, each aspect of the city offers a new perspective and a chance to connect with the Dutch way of life.

Travel is about more than sightseeing; it's about engaging with the local culture, understanding its history, and creating meaningful memories. Amsterdam provides a canvas for such enriching experiences, whether you're indulging in its culinary delights, exploring its artistic heritage, or simply enjoying a moment of tranquility by the canals.

Each season in Amsterdam brings its own charm and a range of activities and events. From the tulip bloom in spring to the cozy holiday markets in winter, the city's seasonal transformations offer varied experiences to visitors throughout the year.

For those concerned about budget, Amsterdam can be surprisingly accommodating. The city offers numerous free or low-cost attractions, and its compact size makes it perfect for exploring on foot or by bike. Embracing the local lifestyle, such as enjoying picnics in parks or sampling street food, can lead to not only savings but also a more authentic experience.

Regarding language, while Dutch is the official language, Amsterdammers are generally fluent in English. However, learning a few basic Dutch phrases can enrich your experience and is often appreciated by locals. Here are some simple phrases to get you started:

▷ Waar is...? (Where is...?)

▷ Hoeveel kost dit? (How much does this cost?)

▷ Spreekt u Engels? (Do you speak English?)

▷ Kunt u me helpen? (Can you help me?)

▷ Ik begrijp het niet. (I don't understand.)

▷ Ik ben verdwaald. (I'm lost.)

▷ Waar is de wc? (Where is the toilet?)

▷ Mag ik het menu zien, alstublieft? (May I see the menu, please?)

▷ Ik zou graag... willen. (I would like...)

▷ Dank u wel. (Thank you.)

▷ Graag gedaan. (You're welcome.)

▷ Alstublieft. (Please.)

▷ Pardon. (Excuse me.)

▷ Hoe kom ik bij...? (How do I get to...?)

Amsterdam's culinary scene is a delightful mix of traditional Dutch flavors and international cuisine. From herring stands and cheese shops to high-end restaurants and hip eateries, the city caters to all tastes and preferences.

In Amsterdam, art and culture are woven into the fabric of the city. The rich tapestry of museums, galleries, street art, and performances is a testament to the city's artistic vibrancy and innovative spirit.

Lastly, take the time to immerse yourself in Amsterdam's unique ambiance. Whether it's a leisurely boat ride along the canals, a bike tour through the countryside, or a quiet moment in a hidden garden, each experience allows you to connect with the city's soul.

With its diverse array of attractions, welcoming atmosphere, and rich cultural heritage, Amsterdam promises an unforgettable journey. It's not just a city to visit, but a place to experience, explore, and fall in love with. So, pack your bags, bring an open heart, and set off on your adventure in Amsterdam, a city that's sure to captivate your heart and leave lasting memories.

Here's to your journey in Amsterdam, a city that will charm and inspire you, staying with you long after your return home.

Final notes

You have reached the end of your journey through Amsterdam, probably one of the most appreciated destinations among travelers from all over the world. We hope that the suggested destinations and our advice will help you plan and enjoy your trip through Amsterdam to the fullest.

The travel guide series of the Journey Joy collection was designed to be lean and straight to the point. The idea of keeping the guides short required significant work in synthesis, in order to guide the reader towards the essential destinations and activities within each country and city.

If you liked the book, leaving a positive review can help us spread our work. We realize that leaving a review can be a tedious activity, so we want to give you a gift. Send an email to **bonus@dedaloagency.net**, attach the screenshot of your review, and you will get completely **FREE**, in your mailbox, **THE UNRELEASED EBOOK**: "The Art of Traveling: Essential Tips for Unforgettable Journeys".

Remember to check the Spam folder, as the email might end up there!

We thank you in advance and wish you to always travel and enjoy every adventure!

Printed in Great Britain
by Amazon

39236157R00108